How to Start a
Christian Daycare

# How to Start a Christian Daycare

## Evangelism & Financial Independence Through Christian Education

Ellsworth E. McIntyre

Nicene Press, Inc.
Naples, FL 34116

© 2021 by Ellsworth E. McIntyre, Ph. D.

All rights reserved.

No part of this book may be reproduced in any form without permission in writing from the publisher. For information, write Nicene Press, Inc., 5524 19th Ct. SW, Naples, Florida 34116

Unless otherwise indicated, Scripture quotations taken from the King James Version (KJV) – *public domain*

Paperback ISBN-13: 978-1-7377-8870-6

Ebook ISBN-13: 978-1-6628-1821-9

"Whosoever findeth a wife findeth a good thing, and obtaineth favour of the Lord" (Prov. 18:22).

Before the world began, the Lord designed the particular helpmeet necessary to support my life's work. With thanksgiving and praise to my God, I dedicate this book to Patricia (Wallace) McIntyre, my wife for 60 years and mother of my eight children—a very good thing indeed!

# Table of Contents

**FOREWORD TO ORIGINAL 1997 EDITION** . . . . . . . . . . . . . . . . . XI

**FOREWORD TO 2021 EDITION** . . . . . . . . . . . . . . . . . . . . . . . . . XIII

**TESTIMONIALS FROM GRACE COMMUNITY SCHOOL PARENTS** . . . . . . . . . . . . . . . . . . . . . . . . . . . . . . . . . . . . . . . . . . . XXI

**INTRODUCTION** . . . . . . . . . . . . . . . . . . . . . . . . . . . . . . . . . . . . XXIX
    Free Men Own Property; Slaves Do Not . . . . . . . . . . . . . . . . . . . . xxix
    Private Property Produces Free Speech. . . . . . . . . . . . . . . . . . . . xxix
    When the American Dream Died . . . . . . . . . . . . . . . . . . . . . . . . . xxx
    Freedom is Ownership, not Prestige. . . . . . . . . . . . . . . . . . . . . . xxx
    The Preschool—Window to Freedom . . . . . . . . . . . . . . . . . . . . . xxxi
    An Inheritance for Your Children's Children . . . . . . . . . . . . . . . xxxii
    A Cesspool of Immorality . . . . . . . . . . . . . . . . . . . . . . . . . . . . . . xxxiv
    Service to God, Family, and Country. . . . . . . . . . . . . . . . . . . . . xxxvi

**CHAPTER I: "THE LABORER IS WORTHY OF HIS HIRE" (LUKE 10:7)**. . . . . . . . . . . . . . . . . . . . . . . . . . . . . . . . . . . . . . . . . 1
    Break the Yoke of Sin and Set the Captive Free! . . . . . . . . . . . . . . 2
    Education is not the Way to Wealth. . . . . . . . . . . . . . . . . . . . . . . . . 3
    Envy and Betrayal . . . . . . . . . . . . . . . . . . . . . . . . . . . . . . . . . . . . . . . 5
    Why Share with the Untalented and Lazy?. . . . . . . . . . . . . . . . . . . 6
    Why Must Teachers Sacrifice? . . . . . . . . . . . . . . . . . . . . . . . . . . . . . 6
    Should Parents Pay Full Cost?. . . . . . . . . . . . . . . . . . . . . . . . . . . . . .7
    Why Should Success Produce Guilt?. . . . . . . . . . . . . . . . . . . . . . . .7
    Profit Should Be a Badge of Honor. . . . . . . . . . . . . . . . . . . . . . . . . . 8
    Christian Marxism Makes Victims of All . . . . . . . . . . . . . . . . . . . . . 8

**CHAPTER II: THE PRICE WE'RE ASKED TO PAY IN PUBLIC EDUCATION** . . . . . . . . . . . . . . . . . . . . . . . . . . . . . . . . . . . . . . . . . 10
    Public Education is Neither Noble Nor Free. . . . . . . . . . . . . . . . . 10
    Complaints Are Fuel to Spend More Tax Money . . . . . . . . . . . . . .11

    In Government, Cooperation is Better than Efficiency . . . . . . . . 12
    Who Chooses the Curriculum?. . . . . . . . . . . . . . . . . . . . . . . . . . . . . 12
    Religious Ideas Are Taught—But... . . . . . . . . . . . . . . . . . . . . . . . . 13
    The Lowest Common Level of Ignorance . . . . . . . . . . . . . . . . . . . 14
    Income Level for Teachers. . . . . . . . . . . . . . . . . . . . . . . . . . . . . . . 15
    The Task of the Teacher . . . . . . . . . . . . . . . . . . . . . . . . . . . . . . . . 16
    High Turnover in the Profession. . . . . . . . . . . . . . . . . . . . . . . . . . .17
    The Retirement Dream. . . . . . . . . . . . . . . . . . . . . . . . . . . . . . . . . 18

## CHAPTER III: THE PRICE WE'RE ASKED TO PAY IN CHRISTIAN EDUCATION . . . . . . . . . . . . . . . . . . . . . . . . . . . 20

    If A Church Board Makes Policy . . . . . . . . . . . . . . . . . . . . . . . . . . 20
    Can the Christian Teacher Discipline Children? . . . . . . . . . . . . . . 22
    Not Jesus of the Bible, But Another . . . . . . . . . . . . . . . . . . . . . . . 23
    If Administrators Make Policies . . . . . . . . . . . . . . . . . . . . . . . . . . 24
    Curriculum . . . . . . . . . . . . . . . . . . . . . . . . . . . . . . . . . . . . . . . . . . 26
    Income Level. . . . . . . . . . . . . . . . . . . . . . . . . . . . . . . . . . . . . . . . . 27
    Low Status . . . . . . . . . . . . . . . . . . . . . . . . . . . . . . . . . . . . . . . . . . 28
    The Christian School May Go Bankrupt . . . . . . . . . . . . . . . . . . . . 29

## CHAPTER IV: LESSONS TAUGHT BY EXPERIENCE . . . . . . . . . . 31

    Loyalty to Church Instead of Fidelity to God . . . . . . . . . . . . . . . . 32
    Never Persecute Other Christians. . . . . . . . . . . . . . . . . . . . . . . . . 33
    Presumption is Sin. . . . . . . . . . . . . . . . . . . . . . . . . . . . . . . . . . . . . 34
    Substituting Church Law for God's Law-Word . . . . . . . . . . . . . . . 39
    Robbing Widows in the Name of God . . . . . . . . . . . . . . . . . . . . . 40
    False Doctrine Leads to Hard Service . . . . . . . . . . . . . . . . . . . . . . 43
    Success Breeds Guilt & Envy. . . . . . . . . . . . . . . . . . . . . . . . . . . . . 44
    More Success Produces Faster Sacking . . . . . . . . . . . . . . . . . . . . 45
    A Golden Parachute to Save from Envy. . . . . . . . . . . . . . . . . . . . 46
    Churchmen Fail to Honor Own Written Word. . . . . . . . . . . . . . . 48

## CHAPTER V: MY ROAD TO FREEDOM . . . . . . . . . . . . . . . . . . . . 50

    Daycare as a Seed Bed . . . . . . . . . . . . . . . . . . . . . . . . . . . . . . . . . 51
    The Idiot Provider . . . . . . . . . . . . . . . . . . . . . . . . . . . . . . . . . . . . 53
    Raised from the Dunghill . . . . . . . . . . . . . . . . . . . . . . . . . . . . . . . 54
    More Success . . . . . . . . . . . . . . . . . . . . . . . . . . . . . . . . . . . . . . . 54

## CHAPTER VI: WHY MY PLAN WORKS ... 56
- Customer is Sovereign ... 56
- Advertising Pays Off ... 58
- Parental Sovereignty ... 58
- Customer Pays a Competitive Tuition ... 59
- Who Has the Need for Our Service? ... 60
- What the Market Really Wants ... 60
- Teacher Is the Owner of the School ... 61
- The Perverted Church vs. the Word of God ... 62
- The More Central the Control, the More Unlimited the Evil ... 62
- How to Keep Schools Decentralized ... 63
- Cost-Cutting is Rewarded ... 64
- Growth of the School is More Rapid ... 65

## PHOTOS ... 66

## CHAPTER VII: THE SECRETS OF SUCCESS ... 83
- Meet a Growing Need: Working Mothers ... 83
- What About Depression? ... 84
- Providing Good Moral Environment ... 85
- Providing Masculine Leadership ... 85
- Genuine Reading Instead of Phony Reading Readiness ... 87
- Children Reading at 3 or 4 Make Very Satisfied Clients ... 89
- Paraprofessional Teachers ... 90
- The Secret of Wealth Creation ... 91
- The Midas Touch ... 92
- The Evil of Silence ... 93
- Religious Persecution ... 94
- Providing a True Education ... 94
- Success Can Be Easily Won by Our Children ... 95
- More Than Conquerors ... 96
- Education for the Real World ... 97
- Sports: A Game Closer to Real Life ... 98
- Add Structure to Add Security ... 99
- Immediate Feedback of Music ... 100
- Lend the Child Your Discipline ... 100
- A Perfect World to See and Hear ... 101

## CHAPTER VIII: WHAT ABOUT GOVERNMENT REGULATIONS? ... 102

## CHAPTER IX: ADVICE ON CORPORATE STRUCTURE ... 105

## CHAPTER X: MY PERSONAL TESTIMONY ... 108
- How the Lord Taught the Gospel to Me ... 109
- My First Religious Experience ... 110
- Off to Church, Pajamas and All ... 111
- Born Again at Thirty ... 114
- Why Was All This Experience Not Enough? ... 119
- Mother Goose Religion ... 120
- The Sermon of a Cold, Stiff Body ... 121
- The Testimony of Converted Drunks ... 122
- "Though I Give my Body to be Burned" ... 123
- How to Find the Lord's Will ... 127
- The Ways of the Lord are Past Understanding ... 128
- The Gospel of the Midas Touch ... 130

## CHAPTER XI: A BETTER GOSPEL ... 132
- More Examples of Gospel Fruit ... 137
- The Holy Spirit Uses Children ... 139
- Families Made Whole ... 140
- The Wyclif Model ... 141
- Waiting Until Six is Forbidding Children to Come ... 143
- Do You Have Zeal? ... 145

## CHAPTER XII: CONCLUSION ... 147
- Why Must You Have a Manual? ... 149
- As in Music, So in Business ... 150
- So, You Have an Education ... 151

## EPILOGUE: GODLY SPOUSES WANTED ... 155

## THE GRACE COMMUNITY SCHOOL APPRENTICESHIP PROGRAM ... 158
- Contact Us ... 159

## MORE BOOKS AND MATERIALS FROM NICENE PRESS AND THE GRACE COMMUNITY SCHOOL APPRENTICESHIP PROGRAM . . . . . . . . . . . . . . . . . . . . . . . . . . . . . . . . . . . . . . . . . . . 160

    Preschool Pioneers Podcast . . . . . . . . . . . . . . . . . . . . . . . . . . . . . 160
    *A Full Reward: Reformation Through Family-Run Christian Schools* by Rev. Aaron M. Slack . . . . . . . . . . . . . . . . . . 161

## GRACE COMMUNITY SCHOOL CURRICULUM AND OPERATIONS MANUAL . . . . . . . . . . . . . . . . . . . . . . . . . . . . . . . . . 162

    Grace Community School Operations Manual . . . . . . . . . . . . . . 162
    College Can Begin at 2 Preschool Curriculum . . . . . . . . . . . . . . 162
    Grace Community School Reading Program . . . . . . . . . . . . . . . . 163
    Grace Community School Math Program . . . . . . . . . . . . . . . . . . 163
    Grace Community School Bible Program . . . . . . . . . . . . . . . . . . 164
    Preschool in a Box . . . . . . . . . . . . . . . . . . . . . . . . . . . . . . . . . . . . . . 164

# Foreword to Original 1997 Edition

About 30 years ago, I predicted to a few audiences that a new and greater reformation was coming, and this reformation would come through Christian schools. For evidence of this, read Ellsworth E. McIntyre's How To Become a Millionaire in Christian Education [This was the original title of this book. Ed.].

The bankruptcy of the state schools is a very obvious one; it is an educational and moral bankruptcy. The bankruptcy of the churches is rapidly approaching a similar level. The churches, where not marked by modernism and unbelief, are antinomian and flagrantly immoral. Their teaching has become pablum, and both Catholics and Protestants know little what their church professes, and the Eastern Orthodox may be worse. Churches insist Orthodox may be worse. Churches insist on faithfulness to themselves, not to Christ, and they cannot command loyalty to a Savior whom they flagrantly disobey.

The Christian school movement has had a frail and rocky history. Dr. McIntyre's account will tell you of the kinds of weaknesses that appear where churches begin schools because of parental demands, which they meet regularly. In spite of this, it is providing us with an educational revolution. As one who has been an expert witness at many trials in court of Christian schools, I know that these schools, for all their faults, are far, far ahead of the state schools. That, however, is not far enough.

But now Dr. Ellsworth McIntyre has demonstrated that children ages two or three to five can learn so ably that they are ready at five for the fourth grade. He has begun a major educational revolution that is going to lead to a new reformation.

His account of his own pilgrimage is both grim and happy reading. It is a commentary on the meaning of wholeness of faith and life. If he does not spare the church, neither does he spare himself. Many people are taught nothing by their experiences; Dr. McIntyre found a graduate course and degree in his.

Make no mistake about it. This simply, honestly written book is a major manifesto, and Christians who neglect its lessons will miss out on our future under God.

— Rousas John Rushdoony
September 30, 1996

# Foreword to 2021 Edition

I first heard about Grace Community School and its apprenticeship program in 1999. I visited Naples, Florida, and met with Pastor Ellsworth McIntyre to learn more about his schools and the apprenticeship program that he offered. I was a young eighteen-year-old fresh out of high school. My first job was working at the local Dairy Queen, and at the time of my visit with Pastor McIntyre, I was working as a station technician for a national talk radio station. Working and making money was a necessity of life. Still, I knew that though I enjoyed the work I did at Dairy Queen and the talk radio station, I knew that these jobs were a means of earning a living and paying my bills, but they were not what I was looking for in the way of a career or calling.

I was able to talk with Pastor McIntyre at length about his schools, how they worked, his vision, and reasoning for starting Christian preschools, and I was able to visit one of the schools and see it in operation. This short visit was both informative and productive. I already knew my community and the world, in general, were in desperate need of moral and academic reformation. My many years of government public school education and private Christian education made me sure of this.

Children all over America were, and are, being systematically stripped of all Christian influence and morality. There is a systematic effort to dumb down education, which produces at best children that graduate from high school believing themselves to be educated because they have been given a diploma, but who are barely literate, struggle to understand basic math, and have no marketable skills at all.

I moved to Southwest Florida and joined the Grace Community School Apprenticeship Program in November of 1999. I went to work straight away and began learning how to teach immediately; the GCS Apprenticeship program is built on practical training and apprenticeship with oversight from veteran teachers and managers. They helped to guide me in learning the craft of becoming a master educator. I found this both exciting and very challenging. What I liked the most was that I was not being taught theory on the subject of teaching; I was being taught how to really teach from day one. I was given a home to live in rent-free for the duration of my apprenticeship (three years). I was paid a full salary, which I was able to save most of during my apprenticeship due to the low cost associated with a single man living rent-free. I was enrolled in an academic program at no cost to myself to help me receive state-recognized degrees such as a CDA and even eventually earned a bachelor's and master's degree in Christian education at no cost to myself. I was licensed to preach by Nicene Covenant Church. Finally, after completion of my three-year apprenticeship, I was ordained to preach by the leadership and elders of Nicene Covenant Church.

As the years moved on, I married my wife Abigail Walker, who was one of the daughters of Pastor McIntyre, and my wife and I ran the Grace Community School in Bonita Springs, Florida. It is hard to explain how wonderful it is to be able to work side-by-side with my wife. Sharing my career and calling with my spouse was not something I had ever thought about doing, nor did it ever cross my mind how fulfilling and rewarding it would be to do so.

It had always been my impression that husbands and wives got along, but if they spent too much time together, it could cause marriage problems. It was a commonly held belief, and liberally stated that you do not mix business and family. Perhaps this was true of non-Christian marriages and families, but not of Christian ones. Working together daily did more to strengthen my marriage more than I could have ever imagined. Over the next twenty years of marriage and working together, we were blessed with eleven children: five boys and six girls. We have now not only managed to work together for the past 20 years, but we were able to completely control our children's religious and educational lives and ensure that they were correctly reared and given a real Christian education. Besides the religious and moral training I speak of, our children from the youngest of ages began helping us maintain our school and eventually became integral to its operations.

As I sit writing this, two of my oldest sons have also begun their official apprenticeship with our school: the same formal training I had undergone years before. However, this formal training is much easier for them than it was for me because of the years and years of experience and informal training they have already received by being at our school each day, seeing us work, and performing the various tasks that they have been given. As an example, my daughter, age fifteen, is already able to handle the full responsibilities of a secretary. She can handle phone calls, knows how to do accounting, and much more. Operating a Christian preschool and business has had many, many personal advantages for my marriage and family.

Lastly, Pastor McIntyre had written a book entitled, How To Become A Millionaire In Christian Education, which I had read before deciding to join the apprenticeship program and had found intriguing. Many people judge a book by its cover; people certainly judged this one. After I read the book, I realized that Pastor McIntyre's vision and purpose behind desiring to start Christian preschools were both evangelistic and practical. He never suggested that Christians should want or work to become millionaires, but rather that Christians could work as full-time missionaries and educators and still make enough money to care for their families' needs.

After twenty years, I can say that it is not only possible in theory to be a full-time missionary and have more than your family needs, but that I have done it. My wife and I have never wanted for anything. We are raising eleven children without worry about not being able to provide from their needs. We own our vehicles and home. We have no debts. And we can save money for any rainy day or emergency that may come our way. More than this, I can't underestimate the impact that my family has had on the children and families that have been in our care over the last twenty years.

God has blessed me in every way possible and in more ways than I believed possible. I want you to be able to say this too, Lord willing. Read on if you wish to know how. You will be inspired and equipped.

— Rev. Jeremy Walker
November 2020

Be careful: this book might just change your life. It did mine.

One man, Pastor Ellsworth McIntyre, wrote this book. It's not just one man's journey; it's the story of his whole family (including my future wife, Amy), who moves towards freedom and a calling and a unique educational facility called Grace Community School. This story just might lead to your own adventure.

God led Pastor McIntyre to an endeavor that has changed and continues to improve the lives of many thousands of students and showed families the path towards financial freedom and a calling in Christian education, with an unparalleled opportunity to make a difference in the world and earn a reward.

We all want to hear, "Well done thou good and faithful servant." We only get a certain amount of time on this earth to do something to make a difference. Your calling is the tool you use to do that. What has God put you on this earth to do?

I've detailed my journey in the book A Full Reward: Reformation Through Family-Run Christian Schools. When my parents came to be apprentices for Grace Community School in 1997, the same year this book, under the provocative title How To Become a Millionaire in Christian Education, was initially published, I had no idea of the impact this ministry was going to make on me.

As I was making plans to head off to conventional college, God drastically intervened in my life, and I became an apprentice at Grace Community School instead. In the past twenty years, I've gotten married and had seven kids with my wife, bought and paid off a house, obtained my master's degree (paid for by Grace Community School), written a book, and become an internet marketing expert managing our schools' advertising.

All this while homeschooling our kids, teaching Bible daily to hundreds of students, and supervising multiple Grace Community School locations here in Southwest Florida.

Another thing: this is a ministry your family will do along with you. I work daily side-by-side with my wife, Amy, and our children. My kids start helping out at our school as soon as they can, teaching reading, working in the office, cleaning, and learning how to deal with people. Every day is an adventure filled with teachable moments. They are learning a practical trade–how to operate a Christian school. As a result, they are showing a level of maturity far beyond what most people think kids of their age should have.

None of this would be possible without Pastor McIntyre's pilgrimage, the details you're about to read. You'll notice the book *is now called,* How to Start a Christian Daycare. *Something similar was going to be the original title until it was suggested a more provoking title might drum up interest. We've gone back to it in an attempt to stay authentic to the central concept.*

*I'm now writing this in the year 2020: it's been almost a quarter-century since this book was originally published. Things seem different, but are they? Epidemics–moral and literal–are out there. Communism fell, but socialism is at our door. Christians focus on the political realm, and churches are weakening. Perhaps most disturbingly, Christians still are not regarding early childhood education nearly as highly as they should.*

*The topics of this book are timeless. The more things change, the more they stay the same. I hope that this reprinting will help a new generation of Christian entrepreneurs to stop thinking small and dare to strive towards freedom and dominion.*

*If you are familiar with R. J. Rushdoony, know that Grace Community School is making practical application of his theology.*

*Grace Community School is the answer to the question, "What is the best way to make the biggest change in society for Christ? "It also answers the question, "How do you take care of your family at the same time? "because the Christian can't do one without the other. 1 Timothy 5:8 says, "But if any provide not for his own, and specially for those of his own house, he hath denied the faith, and is worse than an infidel." Those of us laboring here in Pastor McIntyre's schools and those elsewhere following his system do not suffer for material blessings. You can become a millionaire in Christian education, but that's not the point.*

*That's not to say doing this is easy. It's tough work, and the Christian community at large won't respect you. "The harvest is plentiful, but the laborers are few." We see people come and ago. A lot of times, people become disillusioned when they come to grips with just how much hard work and long days are required.*

*We've seen people fall away. It certainly isn't for everyone. But, if you can do it, it's worth it.*

*This book is more relevant now than ever. I'd like to say that the Christian community has come to its senses in the years that have gone by, but I'm not so sure. The original back cover of this book said it would show the reader, "How to oppose entrenched evil in this world without resorting to politics or guns." Note that this isn't how things are typically done. Those of you looking towards political salvation will be disappointed. I hope that you, dear reader, are prepared to have your presuppositions challenged.*

*R. J. Rushdoony, in his book* The Philosophy of the Christian Curriculum, *wrote, "Humanism in the modern era has had a very simple and effective plan for conquest, control of education. By taking custody of the child's mind, it has effectively determined the future for the past century and a half. It has so thoroughly dominated education that even most of its enemies are extensively conditioned by the basic doctrines of humanism." (I could quote many passages from here at length–it's an excellent introduction to deliberate Christian education)*

*The war being waged against Christianity was once covert. It is now in the open. Think of all the bad things going on in our society. I don't need to name; you know what they are, and the day's flavor is continually changing. Things that would have seemed unthinkable at one point but are now considered mainstream. These developments blindsided many Christians. Consider that despite appearances, none of these things came about because of politics. Nor were they done at the point of a gun. They were done through education, specifically early childhood education. This is the tool Christians refuse to use. Christians are still focused on winning souls at the adult level. We're still refusing to let the little children come.*

*So, is the message of this book still relevant? More so! Many people see the success of Grace Community School but fail to understand the why of what we do. The enemies of Christianity understand how important education is. Children are the key. If you want to make a difference for Christ, no ministry has more of an impact on the future than the Christian preschool.*

*We at Grace Community School have been starting and running Christian preschools for more than thirty years. We haven't given up, and we're still looking for Christian men and women who want to earn their full reward in service to the King. Maybe you will join us. We're in this for the long run. Are you ready to join the battle? Keep reading to see how.*

— Rev. Aaron M. Slack
November 2020

# Testimonials from Grace Community School Parents

In the now thirty-five years since the founding of Grace Community School, we have expanded to seven Southwest Florida locations (with more on the way), and thousands and thousands of students have gone through our programs. Pastor McIntyre's ministry has tremendously benefited the lives of so many students and families. In light of this reprinting after so many years, we decided it would be appropriate and beneficial to include a selection of testimonials (some taken from Google reviews) from Grace Community School parents. *Ed.*

*"Grace Community School has been our saving grace, so to speak. My granddaughter has been there for 3 years and will be graduating from Kindergarten this month. She can read, recite the pledge of allegiance, say prayers, and the 10 commandments. She's been in the karate, dance, art, and music classes and loves them all. I love the family feel you get when you enter, and how they really seem to understand kids. It's been perfect for us, and I thank you for all you have done."*

— Debbie Collins

*"Grace Community has become more than a school; they are all family to our children and us."*

— Megan Sanford

"We love Grace Community School. When my son turned 6 months old, I decided to look at options for daycare. I had seen signs for GCS and did some research. Everything in their handbook sounded right in line with our values. My husband and I stopped in for a visit and were blown away. Happy kids everywhere, teachers treating kids like their own, a clean facility and the food delivery truck had just arrived, so we saw the display of healthy meals our kids are fed. We signed up and have now been there 8 months. Our son is in love with GCS. Getting him dressed each day is so much easier when I can say, 'we're going to school.' He loves all the activities, dance parties, recess, and theme days. We as a family couldn't be happier."

— Justine Bowker

"We enjoy sending our little girl to Grace! She loves going to school every day. The staff is very attentive, and the facility is clean. She learns letters and numbers before pre-k. We also appreciate that she gets Bible Time. A great school!"

— Deanne Boozer

"Great school (not daycare!). My daughter is 3 and already knows her colors and how to count to ten, which I think is a great accomplishment! The hours work perfectly for my husband and I as we need to be at work by 7 and sometimes don't leave until 5. It's truly accommodating to a working family. The weekly payments are very affordable as well! All the fun weekly themes and different parties are a plus as well. She loves it! Our other daughter went here and knew how to read before going into kindergarten which helped put her at the front of the class. We are grateful for everything this school does."

— Autumn Caldwell

"I am now sending my second child to Grace Community. My wife first found this school after carefully going over the pros and cons of many other daycares in the area. While I have two daycares within a mile of my home, my wife chose Grace that was two cities down the road because of all that was being offered at Grace Community School. I could not be happier with her choice as I have seen how my son has grown both in his Bible knowledge and the educational head start he has received. I am sure my daughter will get the same head start both with schoolwork as well as with a bible-based head start. Keep up the great work."

— William Watson

"Great place, very warm and family-oriented. The whole staff feels like family. Would highly recommend this school. I wouldn't send my child anyplace else."

— Vincent Salus

"Being new to the area, I wanted my kids to be somewhere they would grow, learn, have fun, and feel safe. I found all that with Grace Community. My kids love all of the staff there. They all play an important role in my children's everyday experience there and I am so thankful for each one of them. I am amazed at how much they've learned and thrived in a short time. I love the foundation on which my kid's education is being established and the values my kids are being taught. It is a great school."

— Lucy Carrier

"Grace Community School has been a true blessing. The staff is attentive, kind, knowledgeable, and professional. They keep us informed each day on how our kiddo is doing. They treat our family like their family. Our little one is 3 and is already starting to read! GCS takes time with all the kids to help them grow into smart tiny humans! We would recommend them to anyone looking for a thorough daycare!"

— Carrie D'Amico

"After a whole year with my kids here they ABSOLUTELY LOVE IT! It was the best decision I could have made for my kids because they needed to be exposed to the school world to prepare them for later and God knows my one and only daughter has always been the most antisocial child alive, but now she literally cries on the weekends because she wants to go to school when she wakes up! Also, my children have learned so, so, so much since they've been here, and they will be here until they age out. Thanks Grace Community! My family appreciates you very much!"

— Denise Huff

"This place is AMAZING! I have all three of my kids there for three years. My youngest started there at 6 weeks and is now three. I have been to a few daycares around and this is by far the best. The staff are very friendly, understanding, and organized. The morning teacher says good morning to all the kids by name individually. They really are the best and always willing to help out without judgment. I highly recommend this place. They even do fun activities during the summer and holidays!!!! The teachers really do help them with reading, talking, potty training, etc. It is a good structure balance of free play and learning!"

— Brittany Flemion

"We love Grace Community School! My daughter attended for 2 years. Now that she is in a new school, we see how advanced she is for her level. She keeps repeating how easy her work is. We took her into the school to get her reading tested and she tested WAY above her grade level, and I know it is all because of what she learned at Grace. We will for sure be enrolling our other daughter as soon as she is ready for school."

— Priscilla Camacho

"I love the teachers and the staff!! Rev. Harrison and his family are amazing and care about all the children! They know every parent and child that walks through that door!! My daughter started going to Grace for pre-k and she barely knew anything she needed to know going into kindergarten. Now she is in the 1st grade reading at almost a 3rd-grade level and I owe it to Grace Community and all their amazing teachers."

— Kasidi Kent

"I love the fact that my son is excited to go to school in the mornings and loves to tell me about his day when we go home. It reassures me that Grace Community is a great school for both of us."

— Scott Kelsey

"I'd like to take the credit for my son's accomplishments in early reading, but the credit goes to Grace Community School. From learning the alphabet song to certificates of accomplishment in recognizing letters independently, my son has been proud to share his reading development with his friends and family. The day after bringing his first early reading books home from Grace Community School, he has been reading to his younger brother and setting an example of excitement for learning. The day he read 'Lego' in the toy catalog I almost burst with pride. Thank you, Grace Community School for giving my sons everything I would wish to provide at home. Even before his third birthday he was reciting his ABC's and listing the vowels and the sounds they make. At age 3 he brought home his first reading books. I thought, 'Oh, that's cute.' But when he picked up the Toys 'R' Us catalog and read the names of the toys, I was blown away! Learning is the second most important factor, aside from safety, in choosing a school/daycare for my children. The early years set the standard and practice for a child's future learning habits. It's hard to list just one thing as the most important thing my child has learned at Grace Community School. I'm so grateful for the subjects he's learning and the social skills he's developed, but I'm most grateful for his love of learning. I'm 100% confident that my sons will have a seamless transition into primary school and have an advantage over other students. The structure of each activity at Grace Community School and the complete focus of every child in the room has surprised me. It's so different than the average daycare, where the kids seem to be left to their own devices."

— Sommer Garcia

"My family absolutely adores Grace Community School. My children have been attending for almost two years, and they have loved every minute of it. I couldn't ask for more caring educators for my girls! The curriculum is top-notch, very creative and they really know how to make learning fun! My oldest was reading within two months of attending this school. My girls come home and share the stories they learn in Bible Time, the art projects made in Art Class, and put on shows from the techniques they have learned in Dance Class. I recommend this school to anyone."

— Ashlee Rundlett

"All three of my kids attended Grace Community School. My youngest one is getting ready to go into kindergarten and he already knows how to read basic words and write his name!!! As a parent, I cannot express enough gratitude to this school for helping our kids get a great start to their education. This isn't just a daycare, it's a family that has an obvious love for what they do. I have MANY photos that they take each week for us parents to keep. As for the teachers, in the years we have been using this school, I have yet to meet a teacher that myself or my kids didn't create a bond with. (Did I mention their teachers stick around because it's a great school?!) The prices are very reasonable and probably the lowest for this type of care."

— Heather Adams

# Introduction

### Free Men Own Property; Slaves Do Not

What does it mean to be free? The author put this question to hundreds of students when he was a teacher. "What does freedom mean to you?" The responses ranged from a vague "Exercising choice," or "Doing my own thing" to "Owning my own home." Home ownership was as close as anyone came to ownership of private property or ownership of one's own business as the key to freedom.

The truism that the control of a man's paycheck equals control over his will seems unknown in America. Even as an adult Bible teacher, I have never had an adult define "freedom" in terms of owning one's own business. I remember my surprise when my college economics professor posed the "freedom" question to my class and then, to our chagrin, lectured that if we were colonial Americans, instead of twentieth-century Americans, we would not have been so ignorant.

### Private Property Produces Free Speech

Thomas Jefferson envisioned that the best of all societies for America would be a network of free and independent farmers. Jefferson shared the dream that men able to support themselves from their farms could stand up to potential tyrants. The colonials had been taught in Europe what economic slavery was all about. As a matter of fact, social class was tied to property. Just pick up any English novel of that period and note that marriage prospects were considered on the basis of their investment income. A gentleman had income from investments without laboring with his hands; the greater the income, the more eligible the man or woman.

In pre-World War I, the United States was a nation of small businesses and farmers, and the room for geographical expansion made for a relatively happy and prosperous time. Many Americans owned their own businesses, and workers knew their boss since most firms were local and simple.

## When the American Dream Died

As a result of the 1932 depression, there was a dramatic rise in antibusiness sentiment. Many observers term this swing to the Left as an era of liberalism. During the late '30s and after World War II, America became a nation of huge corporations and large chain operations. Government operations, union activity, and declining free enterprise meant that most citizens became wage earners dependent upon a faceless, distant and cold corporation. The idea of owning one's own business and controlling one's own destiny was in eclipse.

## Freedom is Ownership, not Prestige

For the few who could remember or inherited family businesses, it has been absolutely true to the degree that one can provide for himself, he will enjoy more "choice," more "homes," more "free time," and all of the other things which are the result of being free financially. A man on a paycheck, even if he is called "doctor," is not as "free" as a "doctor" with an independent practice. A grocer working for a paycheck from a national firm can be fired tomorrow; a grocer who owns his own franchise or business is free. An executive working for a paycheck is not as free as an owner. Lee Iacocca found that out when Henry Ford fired him. In his book, he whined about Ford's not really owning Ford Motor Company, since it was a public stock corporation; but the truth was that both Henry and Lee were employees of Ford Motor. Henry was more free in that he controlled more voting stock through his family. The man who owns and controls has greater freedom than an exalted executive politician (President of the United States) or a professional on a payroll, such as a school teacher or a minister.

So, the best way for any individual to be truly free is to own his own successful business. Any salaried job or profession is an ephemeral sham, which holds one in bondage subject to the whims and desires of others. If the business one owns can be beneficial, moral and uplifting, so much the better.

If you are reading this, you probably already know the vagaries of salaried employment. When you work on salary for another person, corporation, church or whatever, you are not really free. There can be dignity in labor, as the Bible points out, but there is also a greater dignity, along with the peace of mind, when you own your own legitimate business, i.e., when you control your own destiny.

### The Preschool—Window to Freedom

This book is an introduction to a new way of life for its readers. You are going to learn how to start your very own private daycare/preschool, something you will own, control, be able to will to your heirs, and something which can act as a powerful force for good in America.

I know, because I have done this. There are presently six Grace Community Schools (daycare centers) open in southwest Florida. Each of the schools generates to me an income beyond my fondest dreams.

When I started to develop the community daycare/school concept, I worked harder than at any other time of my life, because I wanted freedom, not the tiresome, humdrum, salaried or commissioned jobs I had held for years. It was not easy. My wife and I lived in a campground trailer for more than a year so that we could devote every last penny we had to start our first daycare. My children sacrificed with us. I must confess that, in the dark of the night, I often came close to despair. Doubts assailed me from every side, but we struggled on. When the risks seemed too high, one thing enabled me to persevere: I wanted freedom for the rest of my life, and the only way to achieve that was to create my own successful business.

The first daycare/school was a success and became profitable sooner than I had imagined possible. We have opened five more since then. The daycare/school concept is a proven success, and it is a success in which you can participate, if you simply display the determination that is necessary.

You can open your own school by using this book and the operational manual as your guide. If you seize your future with both hands, you will better your own life and the moral and educational lives of future Americans.

## An Inheritance for Your Children's Children

I well recall the day our first school crossed into the black, just three months after we built it. I was sitting outside supervising the playground activities of the children on a beautiful Florida spring morning. The morning sun warmed me as I watched the youngsters at play. I was comforted by the thought that no one could ever take my job away from me. No one could ever tell me what to teach. No one could take my old-age security from me; the business was my pension. No one could disinherit my children. My business would continue beyond my death, if my children choose to keep it going. The building was mine, the land was mine, and the clientele was mine. I was free—a true professional for the first time in my life. What a wonderful, thrilling joy! I want that for you. I want you to accumulate an inheritance for your children's children.

Today I have a penthouse condominium, a boat, cars, a big salary—all the material things most people want… but none of this is most important. What is important is that I control my own financial destiny. There are few situations in the world to equal the freedom of financial independence. Financial independence and control are to be greatly sought by thoughtful men and women. But controlling one's own financial destiny with all its attendant advantages is only half the real vision … perhaps less than half.

Every reader who chooses to open and operate his own daycare/school will contribute in a genuine way to the greatly increased educational and moral values of future Americans. This is not a generality, because the American public educational system is failing. This is not news, but rather a generally accepted fact. Each year our grade schools, high schools, and colleges produce students who score lower in standardized tests which have been used for years. When compared to their counterparts in Germany, Japan, England, and in fact any modern, industrialized society, American students do poorly. Their trend is downward.

## A Cesspool of Immorality

Some observers blame the students for this poor showing. The older generation tends to say that the younger generation is not "up to snuff." "Youngsters today don't work or try as hard as we did." Can anything be more ridiculous? It is not the students who are at fault. We are teaching today's youth the wrong things in the wrong way. Even after four or five decades of degenerating scholastic achievement, no better system has appeared on the horizon.

Equally important to declining educational performance is the nearly total loss of moral, ethical, and religious instruction. To be blunt, our public school system is, at best, a failure in teaching how to live a disciplined life. At worst, the public school system is a cesspool of immorality, which dooms a large number of students to live lives of alcoholism, drug addiction, sexual depravity, lawlessness and near illiteracy.

Everyone seems aware of this, but nobody seems to know what to do about it. Of course, the federal government, the major player in creating the public school disaster, almost yearly develops "new" programs to improve our schools. Some "experts" say public school teachers should be paid more, that classes should be smaller, and that yearly operating budgets increased. The list of quick fixes is endless. Yet each year our schools turn out students of lower quality than the year before. The downward trend has been underway for a long time. Still the government, unions, publishers, and local bureaucrats seem dedicated to this deteriorating educational system, which has been proven second rate by years of declining scholarship.

Surprisingly, a small group of young people attend public schools and come away as bright students able to compete with the best in the world. The children of newly arrived Asiatic families are standout public school students by any standard. How can that be? The young Asians come to America with a strong allegiance to family and tradition. They attend public schools and excel, but are also taught discipline and respect for family authority. To the professional observer of our sad public school system, there is little doubt that by the time the second or third generation of Asiatics passes through our present public school system, Asiatics will emerge just as poorly educated as their Occidental neighbors.

It is the author's opinion and experience that, sadly, no one in either governmental or educational life has the genius for turning around the public school system. It is too firmly in place. Many people simply do not know the depth of the situation. If they do know, they feel helpless to improve it. No one wants to pay more taxes to experiment further with an educational system that has already been experimented to near death.

The author believes that there is no way to reform the public school system. There is hope, however, in Christian education. For years, the author experimented with Christian training. In time, it became clear that one could open and operate a daycare/ school that was really that: *a school*. Young boys and girls from ages of two through entry into kindergarten could be shepherded into a secure daycare environment, and could be educated painlessly, even pleasurably, by using the traditional teaching techniques that were abandoned in the 1930s. *It can be done*. It is being done right now in the author's home state of Florida. Daycare/schools are open, operating at a large profit, and are turning out pre-kindergarten students who read at the second through fourth grade level as determined by nationally known and accepted testing methods.

## Service to God, Family, and Country

When one opens a daycare/school, he not only renders an invaluable service to God and America, but he also can become really rich. As this book is written (1996), the author has six schools open. The six operating schools provide gross income in excess of $400,000 per year. If that isn't rich to you, it is to the author. You can achieve this, too.

This book will take you step by step through the process of opening and operating a daycare/school, speedily and profitably. When you have one school open and running smoothly and profitably, you can open a second and then a third. Once your daycare/school is operating, you will be producing educated children, firmly established in the traditional teaching methods. Even more importantly, you will have the opportunity to teach young souls the Christian way of life. You can do it before the public school system gets its hands on the youngsters. Your daycare/school will teach phonic reading, traditional mathematics, recreational and social functioning, music appreciation, computer literacy, and understanding art, along with daily prayer and Bible study.

*You can do it.* The author did it, and he is dedicating his life to helping you do it. Journey with me through the following chapters and change your life for the better as well as the lives of countless young Americans.

CHAPTER 1

# "The Laborer is Worthy of His Hire" (Luke 10:7)

To all serious Christians, . . the laborer is worthy of his hire" is a very familiar Bible verse. When pastors and school boards gather to set wages for Christian teachers, however, there is another verse that is quoted, "My God shall supply all your needs" (Phil. 4:19). This verse is usually delivered by an interviewer smiling broadly with charming, crinkled eyes, not unlike ex-President Jimmy Carter, and in a seductive voice, artificially pronouncing the endings of the words, who says, "Now the Lord has promised to provide not our 'wants,' but only our 'needs.'" Should the candidate for a teaching position be reluctant to name a figure low enough to suit the churchmen, a sermonette follows, whose substance is along these lines, "If, dear teacher, you practice faith and by faith live on less than those lacking in faith, financial miracles will make up for all deficits. In response to your prayer, faithful school teacher, people may knock at the door with gifts in their hand, saying, 'The Lord told me to give this to you. Here is $35.14.'" Marvelous! Just the right amount to add to your pittance to buy heat for your family for next week. No doubt, by earnest prayer, you may have enough next week to buy shoes for that athletic boy.

Yes, in soothing tones, the crinkled, smiling churchman assures the school teacher, "Life can be a new and exciting adventure of faith! God will reward you, because the 'workman is worthy of his hire!'"

## Break the Yoke of Sin and Set the Captive Free!

Seriously, let me confess that I have been on both sides of the teacher-hiring table, and the verse, "The laborer is worthy of his hire," is not always used as the Lord intended. But please don't misunderstand me. The smiling churchman is not a deliberate con man trading on the teacher's relative youth and idealism, but taking advantage of the teacher's youth and idealism is exactly what is done day in and day out. Churchmen are locked into a system that requires an unworthy pay for a worthy workman. The heavy yoke of this system should be broken to set both the oppressed teacher and the captive churchman free. The purpose of this book is to introduce you to a system that has set me free. I have experienced this freedom, and with great pleasure, I happily present a way to *teach without starving!* The yoke of oppression has been removed from me, and I pray that you will learn from this book how the yoke can fall from you.

Eleven years ago, in April 1985, I cranked down the front lift on my ten-year-old, 18-foot Shasta camper. The New Hampshire frozen concrete-like earth needed no wooden block to support the puncture of the pipe cranking down from the tongue jack. The pipe hit the ground and skidded a few inches. In my 1979 Ford station wagon were six of my eight children. I would leave behind for a while (I hoped) the two oldest who were married. I had in my pocket my severance pay and a hope in my heart that I would never work again in any school system, public or private. I had long ago deliberately chosen against the government schools as an impossible system for investing my life's labor. Now, I had sadly finished my last assignment in a

Christian school system. I glanced at the home I was leaving behind, turned my back on the wagon of giggling, squirming, and excited children and fought for control of my emotions. "Finish cranking it down," I ordered my teenage son. "I want to check that the wheels are blocked. The trailer is slipping on the ice. Keep your body clear in case it slips."

My son nodded. The instructions were unnecessary since he had hooked and unhooked that trailer from New England to Florida and from Washington, D.C. to California. The trailer had served for all three of my Christian administrative positions. We had parked that trailer in Maryland, North Carolina and New Hampshire. The first trip was cross-country from Washington, D.C. to California, where we camped with all eight of our children in the San Fernando Valley, while I completed the course work for my doctorate in education. Five girls bunked up inside with my wife and me. The three boys slept in a tent outside the trailer. Traveling during the day, they sat on padded benches in the back of the sturdy 1973 International pickup truck that served faithfully for more than 100,000 miles of service. In a cardboard box at my wife's feet in the cab of the truck rested Abigail, our still-nursing youngest child.

We saw our country "up close and personal." It was a happy period in spite of its hardship. My wife and I still enjoy telling friends about that trip. We laughingly called ourselves, "Okies for Christ," after *Steinbeck's Grapes of Wrath*. But ours was not a trip of despair as was the victims of Oklahoma's Dust Bowl.

## Education is not the Way to Wealth

We had hope and faith that a doctorate would open great doors of financial security and Christian service. That dream was soon shattered! We learned that when my doctoral dissertation was rejected because of political incorrectness, academic letters signify acceptance more than scholarship. Eventually, I would get my Ph.D., but it would be from a Christian institution, instead of a humanistic one.

My dissertation described the learning differences between students in a coeducational classroom versus those in a same-gender classroom. Studies seemed to indicate that boys suffered more than girls from a coeducational classroom. However, when I divided my Christian school into boy/girl classes, we found that girls, not boys, were the victims of coeducational education. This truth was especially unwelcome at that period of our nation's history, because the feminist movement was at its hysterical height. Years later however, when it suited the feminists to try to preserve all girls schools, the University of Southern California did use my ideas but that was too late for me to take advantage of the new vagaries in political correctness.

The Ph.D. is an impressive credential especially for those on the Left and it gives fury to my academic opponents that I have that degree. However, let me point out to the reader that the designation of "millionaire" is to be preferred. Letters after one's name do not have much economic value in a free market. Only in an artificial, scholastic world do such degrees have value, and then only to those who, at least by silence, endorse anti-Christian doctrines. My church-related Ph.D. has had political value in fighting against liberal hypocrisy, but that doesn't put bread on the table.

It is amusing to me that one news reporter exhaustively tried to label my degree as a phony because it came from a church institution instead of a secular. During our interview, I pointed out to the reporter that I did have a secular Master's degree from Georgia Southern that was completed at Johns Hopkins University and that all of the classroom work for my doctorate was done at the University of Southern California. I also had a fully valid transcript to back up my claim. The reporter went away sad but then returned triumphantly with the name of one of the officials of the school that granted my Ph.D. Unknown to me, this official had been convicted by federal authorities for tax problems and something involving failure to properly register church bonds. The reporter was not happy when I laughed at him and asked why this man's current problems, a decade after I received my degree, be of any consequence.

I have said all this to illustrate that academic degrees are more political than academic in our country. To paraphrase the comedian, I have been a scholar and I have been rich and rich is better! Follow the McIntyre system of building your own Christian school and you can laugh at pretentious academic nonsense.

My graduate professors used to refer to the doctorate as a "union card." They were very close to the truth, because no free market would pay a professor for what he does. There has to be a very strong union to guarantee wages to most professors. The professors used the term "union card," however, as a humorous form of good-natured self-depredation. They wished the audience of aspiring doctoral candidates to see them as very modest "good guys," somehow working in league with "working stiffs." Marxism runs deep on America's campuses. So does self-delusion, since most working stiffs share few of the social Marxist values of most college professors.

## Envy and Betrayal

At our departure from New Hampshire, I glanced over the frozen New England pond that had been a backdrop for hours of reflection and prayer. I was angry but not bitter. Odd, I thought, how different from the first time I had been sacked. It had taken me months to overcome the bitterness. All of the schools under my leadership had increased in enrollment. Threatening deficits had been turned into surpluses of over $100,000 annually under my leadership. My reward was envy and betrayal. I was forced to sell automobiles on one occasion for six months until another administrative post opened. During my exile from teaching, I had inevitably questioned my career choice and the direction of my life. The questions swarmed like fish eating one another. Gradually, only four big fish remained—four big fish that had to be landed to make a success of my life as an educator. These were four big questions I struggled to answer.

## Why Share with the Untalented and Lazy?

The first question was, "Why shouldn't good Christian teaching be profitable?" In other professions, the best reaped the largest rewards. In sales, for example, it is known that ten percent of salesmen earn 80 percent of the commissions. Ninety percent live on the remaining 20 percent of the money. I loved that rugged world of instant reward and punishment. It was clear-cut. There is no doubt about winners and losers in sales. Those who have the talent and courage to work harder than others earn the biggest portion of the pie. Why was it in teaching that winners have to share the rewards equally with the untalented and lazy?

## Why Must Teachers Sacrifice?

The second big question was, "Why so little sacrifice by others in the school contract?" In other words, why should the teacher be asked to sacrifice more than the church, or the school, or even the parent? We certainly do not expect similar sacrifices of physicians and lawyers. Why does the Christian teaching profession demand sanctification by starving while other professions reap sanctification by demonstrated competence?

## Should Parents Pay Full Cost?

In my reverie, the third question appeared obvious. "Why shouldn't parents pay full costs?" Parents were expected to pay full costs for food, clothing, and shelter for their offspring. Certainly, medical costs do not spare the patient. Why, when it comes to education, is the professional Christian educator expected to sacrifice? After all, the students are not the flesh and blood of the teachers. Such a question, if expressed in polite company, is met with scorn. "Teachers are sainted by such selfless labor," seems to be a prevailing myth. Really? Is not the laborer worthy of his hire? 'If a man provide not for his own, especially they that be of his own household, he is worse than an infidel and has denied the faith" (I Tim. 5:8). In that passage of Scripture, it is the parent, not a hired teacher, who is charged with providing for his own.

## Why Should Success Produce Guilt?

The fourth question was profound, "Why should financial success produce guilt?" In my three administrative positions, I had demanded and earned $32,000, $34,000 and $39,000 respectively. These are not large sums by any standard except in Christian circles. The dean of my school of education called my salary "exorbitant." I explained in writing to my offended dean that while it was true that my predecessors had been paid less than $20,000, the schools under their leadership had run deficits year after year. On the other hand, I piled up surpluses year after year. As a consequence, I believed my predecessors to be expensive. Since they apparently could not or cared not to earn a profit, their salaries were exorbitant and not a bargain like mine.

## Profit Should Be a Badge of Honor

It is very sad to note that in Christian education, profit is believed to be at someone's expense. Profit must necessarily be robbed from some victim, according to the Social Marxism lurking in academia. The truth is that my Christian schools charged less tuition than other private schools. At lower tuition, my Christian schools still produced a better-educated student. The teachers earned more than teachers in similar competitive schools. In short, there were no victims, but there was the wounded pride of the envious, who cannot make even a small profit. Profit, if legal and moral, should be proof of accomplishment.

## Christian Marxism Makes Victims of All

Once upon a time, I had regretted not entering Christian service before the age of thirty. I had heard, been told, and nearly believed that my years spent as a businessman were "spiritually wasted years." But those years taught a better moral system, based more firmly on the Bible than most Bible colleges and churches. In the marketplace, the tyranny of the profit-and-loss statement allows no room for classroom incompetence and misunderstood Bible doctrine. An honest business does not make a profit because someone has been victimized. Nearly all schools—public, private, and Christian—make victims of teachers, students, and parents, precisely because many believe that one cannot profit and still be an ethical, moral Christian.

Those who are blind to the value of a good steward become wicked oppressors. The just steward who meditates on the law of God (Psalm 1), on the other hand, blesses and prospers all he touches.

Using this hard-earned truth of the marketplace, God has lifted me and my family out of poverty and into the upper 1 to 2 percent of our nation's wage earners. Today, I am a millionaire. God made me so in spite of a flawed education, despite a flawed religious system, and in spite of my own flaws. I sincerely believe that we should confess our faults one to another. Such confession will be painful to me, but it is an act of love. For I am putting feet to my prayer that you will benefit from my experiences and become a millionaire. Read on. Lift up your weary hands. This book will lead the way to a land where Christian teaching does not mean starving.

CHAPTER II

# The Price We're Asked to Pay in Public Education

## Public Education is Neither Noble Nor Free

Public, or more properly government education, is widely and mistakenly believed to be noble and free. In some parts of the Bible Belt, public schools once rivalled motherhood in veneration. To criticize public schools in Texas, for example, is to ask for a black eye. One would suppose that the same government that cannot be trusted to build roads or run a post office without scandal and waste becomes infallible when teaching the young. But the reality of declining literacy has lately crashed against this traditional mindset. This teacher wonders, "How long, O, Lord!" before some Christians cannot ignore the message?

Public education is expensive. Ninety percent of local property taxes is spent on declining, incompetent, unproductive schools. They are no bargain at any price. I know that we must pay taxes, but surely we do not have to use silly excuses like, "Well, our schools are not as bad as some others!" That others have lost more should not be a comfort. In economics, there is a doctrine called "value of opportunity." If our money is not in the best place to earn more, then there is a cost. There is an old proverb, "You can't dance with all the girls at once." You must choose. Opportunity is limited. After all, your children have only one youth. After years have been wasted in a bad choice of schools, the lost opportunity cannot be recalled. Every school, whether it charges tuition or pretends to be as free as the public school, has a very high opportunity cost. Your child has only a few years of childhood.

What is the cost of producing a self-righteous, egotistical child who cannot read or be trusted to give correct change for a Big Mac? Such a failure is very expensive! America spends more per student than any other nation to produce a student more ignorant than every other nation in the First World. What is the remedy according to the National Education Association? "More money! Give us money for smaller classes and bigger salaries." Neither remedy works.

## Complaints Are Fuel to Spend More Tax Money

Who chooses impractical courses? Who decides year after failing year to retain a thoroughly discredited reading system? Who mindlessly decides to teach discredited modern math? Who decides to reward failure with promotion? Who refuses to pay teachers on the basis of merit? The parents? No, my friend, policies are not set by parents. Parents pay taxes to the government, and the government pays the teachers. The piper that calls the tune is the one who signs the checks. The parents' money passes through too many hands. The government administrators choose the policies for political reasons. The politicians do not think in terms of improving results as much as they think in terms of spreading government jobs. The more people on the payroll, the more successful the politician. Complaints about the schools are actually welcome, because complaints create very splendid opportunities to add a layer of new administrators to install a "new program" that will, of course, require more money for more people. Public administrators are almost always poor managers, but poor management is welcome. Why? Because inefficiencies are opportunities to hire new people to put in new programs to "make things better."

## In Government, Cooperation is Better than Efficiency

Not only are public school administrators, as a rule, poor managers, they are poor teachers as well. Why? Do you know which teacher is most likely to be promoted to principal? The coach... that's right, the athletic director. I had two coaches as teachers in my public high school. One taught government; the other, health. Neither seemed to be able to prepare lessons, but both were very popular and likeable fellows. They smiled often. They liked and were liked by their associates. They could be counted on to propose no radical ideas such as merit pay for testable results. They were team men. They were able to play to enable their political bosses to win. In any political organization, cooperation is a great virtue. Promotion follows slavish obedience. Stand outside the graffiti-covered walls of the huge public school palace, and one can almost hear the back scratches and contented purrs of the contented bureaucrats. There is only one sound, however, that will be neither heard nor heeded in the government school—the voice of the parents.

## Who Chooses the Curriculum?

The public classroom teacher may reason, "OK, the system is unresponsive, but when the classroom door swings shut, I can still teach what I want, can't I? Even if my virtue will be neither noted nor rewarded, I will rise above it and gloriously teach!" Fully fired by such noble thoughts, the selfless educator picks up his curriculum, his books and materials. What does he find? A wide choice of textbooks? Sorry, such choices have been made from above. By what standard? Well, there is cost, always cost, and, of course, the paramount question is always, "Does this textbook offend anyone?" Politicians, ex-coaches, and failed teachers have put their collective heads together to guarantee that only the "approved" material enters the classroom.

### Religious Ideas Are Taught—But...

The curriculum is certain to teach several bedrock humanistic, ideas. First, that there are no absolutes. Second, that there are no rules. Third, that every man is entitled to his own opinion of right and wrong. Fourth, that every man is as good as every other man. Fifth, that any man who believes some men are more gifted than others, or who believes that one kind of sex relationship is more moral than another, or that men and women are different, or that private property is superior to socialism, or that one religion is true and others false, is a *bigot!* Above all, every child must be taught to hate and evade being called a bigot. The child must be taught to make no judgments in science except on hard facts. In the science lab, he must ruthlessly judge only on what he can see, hear, touch, taste, and smell. He must be able to reproduce the results, or they are not scientifically reliable, proven facts. However, in all social relationships concerning home, church, government, and business, no amount of demonstrated, reproducible evidence of hard facts must be permitted to sway his faith in the equality and brotherhood of man. Men, women, perverts, saints, sinners, criminals, and all shades and variations must be valued equally. When the student can value the criminal's rights, the homosexual's rights, the infidel's rights, the failure's rights as equal to or greater than his own, he is pronounced "educated." If, however, he junks the tenets of the humanistic faith to recognize the obvious, that all people are not equal, he will be punished for blasphemy against the high gods of the public school.

Make no mistake: children should be taught that all men are equal under God's law. That is to say, God respects no man's person. God will punish sin according to His law. Instead of teaching Biblical equality, however, the public schools teach no law, no rules, no faith, no values, and will not teach these, I suppose, until there will be a freeze in a Southern region; but such a humanistic worldview does not change reality. God values men on the basis of His law-word and it is blasphemy to teach any other standard (See R. J. Rushdoony's book, *Institutes of Biblical Law, Vol. I*).

## The Lowest Common Level of Ignorance

Regrettably, the most idealistic, well-meaning teacher can never overcome the curriculum straight jacket and the pervasive anti-Christian religion of government schools, but suppose for the sake of argument that God's law could be taught as binding for a successful life and that in economics and history, government could be judged on testable results, would the curriculum be acceptable? Hardly, for another crippling reason: the curriculum would still fall of its own weight. Textbooks have to be written to be sold in all fifty states. The text that survives the lowest common denominator lands in the classroom. No textbook can be used that reads above the national reading level (fifth grade and falling is the current level). The student, who learns from such a text, is sure to sink or tend to sink to the lowest standard of the lowest state. That is a standard too low for this teacher. What about you?

## Income Level for Teachers

It has become a byword that teachers are underpaid, but to suppose that raising teachers' salaries would automatically raise teacher performance requires humanistic faith in the face of scientific reality. People are rarely motivated primarily by money. Power, prestige, and recognition mean much more than money to most people. Most truck drivers make more money than school teachers, but which would most mothers prefer their children to be? Let's suppose, for the sake of argument, that money could motivate most teachers. How are we to reward the best teachers? Remember, most teachers, with a great and unshakable faith, believe that all are equal in all respects. After all, they teach this daily in all that they do. They live by democratic majoritarian notions. If the government decides that one teacher has more value than another, what will happen to their ethical system? It would be a brave but foolish ex-coach/ administrator who dared to install such a merit system. Since the public political system punishes such bravery and rewards egalitarianism, you can be sure the public school will be invaded and captured from the outside before an unequal pay system can be installed from within. What passes as a substitute for merit pay are pay increases for completing graduate courses. Graduate courses have no power to bestow or reward God-given teaching talent. Master's degrees and doctorates are equally as powerless, as are four-year undergraduate degrees, to raise teacher performance. Pay raises for graduate study are very popular, because graduate study requires more government jobs, more money, and more power for politicians.

Sadly, throughout my lifetime of 61 years, the status of teachers has declined. The *mala dictum*, "Those who can, do; those who can't, teach, and those who can't teach, teach teachers how to teach," has become painfully more true than ever before. I can still remember my shock when my English professor at the University of Pittsburgh commented, "If a man can write, he doesn't want or need a professor like me to teach him, because if a man can write, he doesn't require a college degree to succeed." The greatest of the creative geniuses, as a rule, do not hold teaching chairs; they are too busy doing.

## The Task of the Teacher

The task of the teacher is to point out what talent achieves and to transmit an appreciation of skill or art to the non-gifted. We can learn to appreciate good music, but no amount of teaching can make everyone into a composer. Only God can make a composer. We can teach economics, but only God can make an entrepreneur. I do not belittle teaching. Teaching is my great joy. The good teacher is a gift of God no less than the composer or writer. If a teacher can open the eyes of our children to see, hear, and appreciate the good, the moral, and the beautiful, he has been successful. Let us not ask our teachers to pretend to be as gods, bestowing talent. Teachers, as a matter of fact, do not have to be doers. They merely need to stimulate, uncover, and discover the talent buried in the child. The teacher who can do this is endowed by God with a gift not to be despised. Unfortunately, many of my teachers not only could not stimulate a child, but they hated and envied all who could. Instead of raising consciousness of beauty and talent, they taught that the great were mere mortals like us. My teachers taught us that we could each become like George Washington, Mozart, Mark

Twain, or Andrew Carnegie. We were just as good, just as equal. Genius, they were fond of cooing, is 99 percent perspiration and 1 percent talent. Is it any wonder that suicide claims so many? How can a teacher who has the gift to teach going to gain recognition in such a system? All men are not equal except under God's law. The gods of humanism, however, stalk the school halls, sniffing for anyone who believes in the law of God to put all such godly teachers into unemployment.

## High Turnover in the Profession

Most newly certified teachers never stay long enough in the system to fully appreciate the ties that bind them to mediocrity. Teaching, for many women, is a brief stop on the road to marriage. Once she has married, then it is exit time for the woman. For a man, bound by matrimony, it is time to get serious about earning a living; consequently, it is also exit time for him. Those who stick to teaching come to accept their relative poverty compared to those of equal educational credentials as "honorable." When they speak, one hears a familiar refrain. The career teacher says, "I could have left teaching, as you did, but I could not be happy doing anything else. I am just as talented as you are, but I have a great and tender heart. Teaching is my life, an imperative written into the biology of my being. I accept low esteem and a low salary. I genuinely hope you are happy not teaching and very, very guilty that you are not a saint as I am. You have renounced the faith in the basic goodness of mankind, and you will be rewarded by the devil with prestige, money, and power. However, I will have my integrity."

## The Retirement Dream

Our humanistic teaching paragon of integrity is not planning to live totally on virtue, however; he has reserved a golden parachute called "the state retirement plan." Since achieving my current financial success, my family has enjoyed five ocean cruise vacations. We thoroughly enjoyed a week or so of absolute luxury in those floating dream hotels. One of the astonishing discoveries I have made on these voyages is how few rich people I have met. No, not even one! Around the table of ten, I have chatted over dinner with my fellow travelers. To make conversation, I introduce myself. "Hi, I am Ellsworth McIntyre. This is my wife, Pat." They answer with eyes, not rising from their plates, "I am Joe and this is Sarah." Very seldom do they give their last names—I wonder why? To keep the conversation going, I will say, "Pat and I are school teachers. We own several private schools in Florida." That usually breaks the ice. A volume of questions about me follows, but still no clue as to who *they* are and what *they* do. When I finally drag from them their names and occupations, I find usually retired local and federal government employees.

Apparently, the business successes do not often cruise. However, I am haunted by a horrible thought. What happens if the state retirement system fails? Do you know how many state retirement systems have failed in the history of the world? Tough question? Well, let's put it this way. How many state pension systems have succeeded? You would be right, if you said, "NONE!" Oh, they spit out money for a while like a pyramid chain-letter scam, but they always fail! When the state retirement pipe dream bursts in the air (not if, but when), the virtue of the priest of the public school system will turn to ashes in his mouth. He who labors in the temple of the public school had better prepare for a poor old age. The winners are out there on the cruise ship now, but they are on the front end of the pyramid scheme. Which end will be yours?

CHAPTER III

# The Price We're Asked to Pay in Christian Education

This book will not be read, I suspect, by many public school teachers. Some may begin, but it will be a hearty heretic of a public school teacher who will get this far into the book. If there is one out there (congratulations!), hang on. I do have a solution. I do have a glorious plan for "teaching without starving." Persevere: your heavy yoke of government oppression can be lifted. I have a wonderful plan for your life!

No doubt the majority of eyes on this page peer out of heads full of Christian teaching dreams. You chuckled through the previous chapter, musing "Amen, brother, preach it to them! Show no mercy! Take no prisoners, slay utterly! They are the bad guys; we Christian teachers are the good guys, right?" Well, brother or sister, there is a price in Christian education also, and we must examine ourselves, first searching for the beam in our own eye before we find the speck in our brother's eye.

## If A Church Board Makes Policy

Who sets the policy in the church school? Who decides what is an education in the church? To paraphrase Mark Twain, "After God made jackasses, he made school boards as an encore."

Churches have school boards. Perched high on these boards are the proud graduates of the government schools.

Almost universally, they seem to have baptized their public school Social Marxist with Christian clothing. They believe in no absolutes ("We are not under law but under grace," they never tire of saying) and no rules ("We will decide by majority vote"). They believe every man is entitled to his own opinion of right and wrong ("That's your interpretation. I read the Bible differently," they say). "I am as good as any man" is the credo of the modern Christian. Since Christians believe themselves not bound by God's law, but under grace, then God must mean to say, "All men are equally sinful or equally good in all respects." Doesn't God say that He is no respecter of persons (Acts 10:34)? Surely, the old-time Christians believed in equality before the law alone and inequality in all other respects; but that was before our modern, enlightened, and glorious appreciation of the equality of man and the unconditional love of God.

Calvin, Luther, Knox, and all the greats had a mean streak in them, according to some modern Christians. These greats did not appreciate how free grace can save a person without any resulting reformation of character. So what if our students in Christian schools fall prostrate before the god of chaotic music—so what if our students act, look and smell like unconverted kids—the important thing is that they know we love them in spite of their sin, just as God does. "Love, that's the answer," is a shibboleth of the modern Christian. When our students turn of their free will from their wrecked lives, they will return to our churches serenely sure that Christ must accept them. Christ must forgive them no matter what. Christ will not punish them. No, perish the thought. To have such a thought is to sin against the grace of God (or so they believe)!

All these perversions of the truth are rooted in Social Marxism. They have no soil in the Bible. Nowhere does our Lord promise to hear the prayer of the sinner at the sinner's choice of time. Instead, our Lord warns, "Call now! Boast not of tomorrow! Today is the day [not a day but *the* day] of salvation." Our Lord nowhere in the Bible invites us to believe ourselves saved while continuing in sin. Instead the Lord warns, "If you love me, keep my commandments." Obedience is the evidence of genuine faith. A profession of faith backed up by a changed life is the bedrock of the real saint. All orthodox

Christians of all ages surely cry out in horror at the notion that heaven can be gained without supernatural reformation. I John 5:2,3 reads, "By this we *know* that we love the children of God, when we love God, and keep His commandments. For this is the love of God, that we keep His commandments and His commandments are not grievous." The author labored for 14 years, from 1971 to 1985, in several Baptist day schools, both as a teacher and an administrator. I found many in secret who would endorse this historical orthodox Christian faith, but always in secret in order to stay employed.

## Can the Christian Teacher Discipline Children?

Faulty theology is not the only defect in most Christian schools. Discipline of rowdy, rebellious teenagers is an unpleasant but necessary task in any school, public or Christian. In a church-related school, the elders' children present very peculiar problems to the Christian teacher. If the elders believe in a God who loves unconditionally, the obedient and disobedient alike, if the elders adore the God who always responds slavelike to the will of the sinner, or if the elders believe that the teacher must always respond in permissive love as does his imaginary God, what will be the fate of the teacher who punishes an elder's child? Will not the Christian teacher be accused of being unchristian? You'd better believe it! If you dare to even raise your voice, the condemning stone of "unloving" will zing against your head, followed by the stones of all the elders as they gather for your execution. True, some parents will still accept punishment for their own kids, but most only believe in punishment for other people's kids. I know the outward expression is, "Spare the rod and spoil the child," but the inward thought is that "My child will never need a paddling."

## Not Jesus of the Bible, But Another

The donors of the church must also be considered. My generation and their seniors are not Bible believers, as a rule.

They attend church in an unholy, craven fear. Death hovers beyond the day, but they know only the name, Jesus. The person behind that name is not the Jesus of the Bible, but another person entirely. The preachers know how to open the hands of the donors. He must preach that "Love is the answer." It is a very old heresy, nothing new.

Chaucer in his *Canterbury Tales* described a foolish plump nun with a badge upon her breast. The Latin inscription on the badge is translated, "Love conquers all." By this, the nun did not mean demonstrated, supernatural obedience to the law of God (I John 5:2,3) but instead, a rosy, toasty, glowing good feeling of affection for her make-believe god who forgives all, always and in response to our will alone. Donors love this housebroken, well-behaved servant-god. This god alone can pry open the greedy hands of the "fat cats" of my generation. Every pastor knows this. If you doubt it, just listen to his sermons! Yes,

yes, yes, there are exceptions, but the holy minority write books, preach sermons, and teach school to a remnant.

The Bible's Jesus is not a friend to this world's churches. If this is so, and it is, then most Christian schools are not the huge improvement over government schools of which they are capable.

## If Administrators Make Policies

Our Christian schools are business enterprises. Does that shock you? Most likely, it does because we are taught to take the "not for profit" label seriously. But what happens to schools which cannot make the payroll? They either go out of business or they beg. My mailbox is heavy with letters from such silly managers. I recall a classic missive that gave me years of laughter. The letter began, "Dear Christian friend, As I write this, the drone of the diesel caterpillar can be heard through my office window. We are clearing ground for our new fellowship hall and gymnasium. We need your help, brother," the letter said. "Summer has come and the tuition from our students has stopped until fall. We were caught short, and our sacrificing, dedicated teachers will not get their final paychecks unless you respond to this plea. Please, please pray, and we are sure...."

What's funny about that? Well, I suppose a school administrator knows the students leave for the summer, don't you? How can that be a surprise? Surely, a manager with an I.Q. above room temperature would be ashamed to write admitting this. What in the world is the caterpillar tractor clearing ground for more building when the payroll cannot be met? If a businessman in the private sector wrote such a letter, he would be committed. I wish such letters were rare and the exception, but they are not. Poor management of Christian works seems the rule, and not the exception. The best beggar is called a "development or stewardship director." The practice abroad in Christian education is to run the school into the ditch and cry for help.

Not only are church administrators poor managers, they are very poor in dealing with parents. For example, nearly every Christian school attempts to impose a dress code on their students. I support such efforts, and I believe a dress code is essential to any school, Christian or public. If a McDonald's fast food restaurant needs a dress code, shouldn't a school? No wise parent should bicker over such a necessity, but there is room for surprise in how such a dress code is enforced. Instead of a polite note mailed home to the parent or a diplomatic phone call, I have seen children publicly tongue-lashed for not meeting the code. When the child gets home crying about her humiliation, the parent is outraged. Why? Simple: the parent purchases the child's clothing, and the parent either cuts the child's hair or takes the child to the barber. Most likely, the parent directs the barber's work. The silly administrator or teacher is inadvertently punishing a parent. Not very smart, don't you agree? Yet some administrators can spend years repeating this mistake. As the apostle wrote, "For what glory is it, if, when ye be buffeted for your faults...." (I Pet. 2:20). I know where these men learned this foolishness. Their college imposed the standards on them, using similar measures, but there is a vast difference between dealing with a dormitory student 500 miles from home and a ten- year-old boy or girl. The child is not autonomous; therefore, the child is not necessarily rebellious when he shows up with long hair. Even if he is consciously rebellious, a wise administrator gets the parent in his corner before trying to straighten out the child.

The Christian teacher needs to remember that his authority is grounded in God's covenant with the parents. To move contrary to the wishes of the parents is similar to a mother and father arguing in front of a child. God has given the child to the parents, and teachers are just substitute parents, deriving their authority from the parents. A good rule for any school is this, "No teacher will speak directly to a student concerning a dress code violation. Instead, the problem is to be referred to the supervisor for appropriate action. The appropriate action is always to consult the parent in private."

Church schools have another flaw to overcome. The best administrators frequently leave for better jobs. Besieged by parents vs. donors, elder's children vs. school parents' children, faculty vs. church staff, financial problems, moral problems, etc., every year many administrators, who would grow into efficient managers, simply burn out. Someone somewhere must come up with a way to teach without starving. I am glad you read that, because there is a better way.

## Curriculum

Let us consider the curriculum of the Christian school. Does the Christian teacher have a greater choice than the public school teacher? Perhaps, but in most cases, personal experience says no. What about the lowest common denominator problem? Well, we still must not offend the Social Marxist Christian; therefore, we must water down the academic content, so more children can transfer from the public school to the church school. But the result is that the student is given a stone instead of bread. The students of the church school usually score better on standardized tests, but not that much better; because the model is not that different. If we would have dramatically superior results, we must have a dramatically superior school model, and that model can be yours!

## Income Level

Like it or not, the Christian school owner faces parents who are not willing to buy his product. The product of the Christian school can be obtained for free at the public school. Because the product is not superior enough to overcome the inferior-free product, Christian education is viewed by the parent as an attractive option, or even a "holy" option, but not as a rule, an irresistible option. "Train them up in the nurture and admonition of the Lord" is not regarded as a binding law. Most Christians believe in the dispensational heresy that God's law is itself an option. R. J. Rushdoony is in the habit of showing up at court proceedings when Christian schools need an expert witness to present the Christian's lawful obligation to get a Christian education for the Christian's children. Dr. Rushdoony is badly needed, because if the fundamentalist were put on the stand, he would be exposed as taking the Lord's commands as "principles" or as "guidelines," but certainly not as binding law. As I heard one Christian attorney put it, fundamentalists have a "preference" for Christian education but not a "conviction." In order to have a conviction, one must recognize a law that cannot be broken. The attorney was too polite to point out to the assembly of Christian educators why they had no law. As a consequence, his doctrine went over the head of the audience. Salvation by faith does not eliminate the law as the standard to measure genuine regeneration.

 Is it necessary that the Christian teacher be asked to sacrifice so much for an inadequate living? Is it necessary that the Christian teacher labor without a retirement program or standard health insurance? As I stated in the first chapter, I have eight children. I had to deliver two of them personally at home. It was a wonderful experience for my wife and me, but what a terrible risk! Why should a Christian teacher be forced to jeopardize the health and safety of his family like that? One of the busybody women of the church spread the word around the church that we delivered our child at home. She did not do it maliciously. On the contrary, she thought it was wonderful. She was sure that I did it to prevent the child from being assigned a social security number, a number which she believed, was the "mark of the beast." With wild excitement, she told how I had defeated the anti-Christ. My high school students peppered me with questions about birthing babies. My answers, I now know, may have been too graphic. Another group arose, (no doubt the plot of the anti-Christ) crying for my scalp: "He's teaching sex education!" they thundered. My principal demanded my dismissal, but my pastor, not always noted for a cool head, overruled the principal to prevent a church split between the believers in the anti-Christ social security numbers and those wishing to fire a sex educator. I kept my job for another year. Substandard health insurance, you see, can have far-ranging and unforeseen consequences.

## Low Status

Not only is the Christian teacher sacrificing a decent living, a decent retirement, and standard health insurance protection, but his status suffers before the parents of his students. The teacher will tell himself that the sacrifice is well worth the price, but what of his wife and children? Substandard housing, substandard transportation, and substandard clothing leave permanent scars on the teacher's children. One day the teacher will ask himself if it is right to ask his wife and children to endure hardship. Women and children will compare their home, car, and clothes to what others have. They will not or cannot long ignore the difference. Try as they may, they will be seen as objects of charity. The parents will send their old hand-me- downs and canned goods. The parents mean well, but one doesn't have to receive such gifts to know that "It's more blessed to give than to receive." When the Christian teacher sees the pain in the eyes of his wife and children, it is a severe assault on his manhood. Is this necessary? Is this the way it must be?

## The Christian School May Go Bankrupt

To the burden of poor job security, no retirement program, substandard health insurance, low status, and becoming an object of charity must be added another cruel, piercing thorn for the brow of the suffering Christian teacher. The school may go bankrupt! Every school that my career took me to was on the verge of bankruptcy. Remarkable to record, every school had no real shame about the prospect of bankruptcy. Financial failure is just not embarrassing for many Christian churches and schools. The general public does not know how extensively the cancer of debt has infected the church.

As a young man of 24, I worked for a trucking company. All of my young life, I had attended church, and I had a high opinion of the institution's integrity. Imagine my anger and surprise when the trucking home office sent down instructions not to deliver any freight to religious institutions on credit. I asked my terminal manager if the president of the company hated churches, or what? Everyone in the office smiled indulgently. Those in business know who the deadbeats are. Such businessmen seldom speak publicly about the churches' "sin," but I must. Christian institutions, as a rule, have poor credit records. Experienced businessmen and Christian teachers should not trust their future to incompetence, especially if it's not necessary.

Using my system, as described in my operational manual, you can place your future in better hands: your own!

# CHAPTER IV
# Lessons Taught by Experience

Must we always learn by personal suffering at the cruel hands of experience? Can't we learn instead from examples, and benefit from the experience of others? Would it not be better if we took the advice of experienced mentors? Yes, unquestionably so, but I am ashamed to admit that some lessons have been beaten into this teacher again and again only by brutal experience.

In the hope that you may benefit by my wounds and avoid my mistakes, hear a horrible (but true) tale of this pilgrim-teacher on his way to a better place where all good Christian teachers can teach without starving.

The road included six hours of searing heat from Greenville, South Carolina to a Baptist day school in Savannah, Georgia. My six children clamored for a cooling turn next to the window of the tiny Volkswagen. The rolling hills of the Piedmont flattened to the endless plain of the Tidewater country. Tall pine trees mixed with something new to our Yankee eyes—palm trees—gave way to the huge, stately oaks draped in Spanish moss, lining the streets of old Savannah. Visions of a subtropical paradise swayed in our minds in concert with the palms fencing Victory Drive.

No more cold Pennsylvania winters, no more meaningless commercial work. We were in the wonderful Bible-believing, conservative South. The promise of freedom to teach our glorious faith was worth any sacrifice, but Savannah was not sacrifice (or so we believed). We were willing to brave any hardship to give the young the benefit of our experience and the Word of God. True, we would have to continue to live in our tin-roofed trailer, but such a price was too small to merit even a passing consideration. We were in the glorious, Bible-believing, sun-kissed South, on the seashore with a golden opportunity to earn heavenly reward. But in material terms, the reward was small. My salary was only $6,000 per year, but that was more than any other Christian school had offered. It was enough.

The swaying palm tree and Southern vision came true for three years. We bought a trailer lot on a saltwater creek behind Savannah Beach. Those golden days yield memories of crab traps, shrimp nets, and the sting of salt water in the eyes. In my mind's eye, I can still see the dolphins playfully leaping high into the air at high tide in my backyard.

## Loyalty to Church Instead of Fidelity to God

Blessings also followed in the classroom as well as at home. 18 of the 32 seniors graduating at the end of my third year of teaching chose to continue their Christian education at my alma mater, Bob Jones University. Then the tin roof of my sunny world collapsed. My alma mater was not the pastor's first choice for his graduates. Angrily, he began to pressure the young graduates to reject their decision to follow my footsteps. When the news of the conflict reached my surprised ears, it was already too late to restore good will. Still, I heroically tried. I became neutral about college choices. My students decided that I was under pressure to keep my job. Too late I realized my feigned neutrality was gasoline on the fires of discontent.

I quietly started looking for a new position. I found one at a large school in Indiana, but my angry pastor levelled charges that I was unfit for Christian work, because of "disloyalty" to the pastor. The Indiana school withdrew their offer. Finally, I found a school that neglected to get a reference from the vindictive pastor. I breathed a sigh of relief. At least I would be able to feed my family. Another job offer came from a local roofing products company. Craftily, I allowed everyone to think I was going to quit teaching when the school term ended and work in a factory. The persecution stopped, I suppose, because my pastor believed that he was successful in driving me from my calling.

The short peace was not to last. My students were heartbroken when their school annual arrived. Proudly, they had dedicated the annual to their beloved teacher. It seemed that they too erred. The angry pastor intercepted the yearbooks and had my picture cut from the book. The pettiness of this deed astonished even usually impassive teenagers. Fearful insecurity crept into the eyes of the students. Many had known divorce in their lives. They had hoped to find higher things from those who teach the Word of God.

My family found their happy times on the seashore ending. It had been a joyful time that even our relative poverty could not dampen. As the wise proverb teaches, "When children are very young, all is well if they are with Mother and Father. They will lie in the gutter with contentment."

## Never Persecute Other Christians

Today in my preschool ministry, I teach many children who have fine clothes and lovely toys. They have houses to live in, but no home so magnificent as a tin-roofed trailer with Mother and Father and no fear of divorce. Among those too familiar with insecurity, the little preschoolers say the heartbreaking things. My wife and I have grown accustomed to fearful eyes.

"Mrs. McIntyre, where is Mr. McIntyre going?" My wife will respond to the fear in the little one's voice and eyes, "To the bank, honey, just to the bank." As the tiny one watches my car depart the school parking lot, the child searches my wife's face and haltingly says, "Is he ever coming back?"

Every parent considering divorce should be required to hear that moan and see those eyes filled with pain. Hopefully, they would not want experience to teach their children to believe in divorce. Likewise, it is horrible to persecute substitute parents or teachers. It hurts the already wounded children of broken or breaking homes. It is enough to know about such things in the world. Such pettiness should not be seen among those called "Christian."

## Presumption is Sin

My teaching career was the first of many church-fight lessons in the blind sin of presumption. My wife meekly followed me without complaint across the polished hardwood floors of our six-year-old brick home past the huge stone fireplace out the door to live in a mobile home park. It would be 16 years before we would know middle-class housing once again.

Not only would we learn to live without a brick house, but without proper clothing (we learned how to use secondhand stores), proper health care (we learned to use the poor clinics), proper food (we learned to use charity); and finally, we even learned to deliver two of our children at home to save medical expenses. We were told by our Bible teachers that all of the above was living by "faith." The Bible, however, has a different name for what we did. It is called "infidelity." In direct opposition to the expressed word of God and common sense, we neglected to provide for our own: "If any provide not for his own, and specially for those of his own house, he hath denied the faith and is worse than an infidel" (I Tim. 5:8).

Biblical love is the keeping of the commandments (I John 5:3). To live in disregard of God's Word is not faith but presumption masquerading as faith. Of all people on earth, the Christian should be the most careful to provide for his family. The Christian, led by He who is faith, has no choice but obedience. It is the *law!* Because my family survived and even prospered spiritually does not prove the correctness of my inadequate theology. What my experience proves is that the Lord generously decided to forgive my sin and reward my blind efforts in spite of my error. What if my wife had died in childbirth without proper medical attention? What if my children had risen up to curse the church that failed to pay their father a decent living? Would my college teachers have blessed my walk of faith under any of the above? Probably, a fool's faith is often secure even in the face of reality and Scripture. I, on the other hand, would not abide in make-believe "faith," because the Lord, by grace, taught me to believe in the more Biblical way. Scripture taught by experience is a lesson not to be denied when taught by the gracious hand of God. My teachers only knew the words, "The workman's worthy of his hire." Today the schools I own pay couples up to $50,000 a year. Why? Because I believe the workman is worthy of his hire. I am bound by His love to obey. This is a stronger faith!

To return to the narrative, however, I had already found a new position. I had only three days of employment remaining. My offending picture had been sliced from the yearbook. Mercifully, burning at the stake is beyond the powers of the modern church, so my punishment for undue influence on my students was complete. Right? Wrong! There's more!

After the Sunday evening service, my pastor blocked my usual exit out the side door. I was startled to see him smiling widely, beaming with what seemed like pure love. "Please stop by the office before you go home," he gently asked. I turned to my wife and asked her to wait, since we only had the tiny Volkswagen and a twenty-mile round trip to our trailer. I pondered what the pastor could have on his mind: "He's a good guy," I thought. "A little hotheaded, but a great Christian. He's smart, at least most of the time. I'll bet he wants to say he's sorry and to wish me well. Sometimes even when staff members stole money or committed adultery, he would find another job for them at another church. My pastor could be most forgiving. After all, I had not been a thief or adulterer. My students had just loved me too much to go to the pastor's college. Yes, that must be it," I thought. "He'll want me not to leave on Friday but stay over for the Sunday service. Sly dog that he is, such a move will heal the church; that is, if I am willing to forgive and forget carving me out of the yearbook. Oh, well, if it helps the church, I suppose I must forgive. Why shouldn't the pastor publicly wish me well? After all, I had lasted three whole years. That was longer than the principal, his staff, and most of the faculty had lasted."

My silly speculations faded into cold reality as the pastor's office door swung open to reveal a room full of twisted, nervous faces. If I am ever to die as did my Lord, I will know the little, impotent stare of small men who will not or cannot bear to look at the face of the innocent damned. As I eyed each man one by one, he looked carefully at the floor. The pastor delivered an angry monologue interrupted by two accusers. One was a parent who testified that his son, who was not present, had once remarked that he thought that Mr. McIntyre did not agree with the pastor's doctrine. The accusing parent was not sure what and where the alleged disagreement was, but the charge was solid enough for my enraged pastor. My questions were only fuel for the pastor's recollections of remarks made by one of the mothers in the church book store. Yes, the pastor was sure now that he remembered a mother, whose son also had doubts about my Bible doctrine. "Oh, yes!" the preacher almost yelled this point. Our fearless church leader had found in the waste paper, taken from my room, student papers which quoted Mao Tse-tung, the Chinese Communist. Eyes bulging, neck chords dancing, he glared at each of the school board. Suddenly, I seemed to notice that the men seemed even smaller than usual—an incredible shrinking band of silent faces. When Elijah asked Israel, "Why halt ye between two opinions?" I now know why Israel "answered him not a word." Israel came to see someone die, and they were not about to see it be themselves! They were spectators, nothing more!

My other accuser was the pastor's alter ego, the youth pastor. He said that I had deliberately scheduled a graduation party at my trailer in conflict with one of his activities. He further remarked that he knew of the conflict in advance and had warned his youthful charges to avoid my party or risk being thrown from the church. In face of this challenge, some of the teens had told the youth pastor to his face where to get off. "Not a very surprising, unexpected consequence for normal teenagers," I remarked. "Why didn't you just let me know of the conflict so that I could change the date of the party?"

The roar of the pastor drowned out the stammering reply of the dull-witted teen leader. "I don't believe you didn't know. Don't try to say that. You did it on purpose. . . ." Taking advantage of a short gap of silence while the pastor gasped for air and new ways to repeat his "serious" charges, I begged each man in the room with children in my classes to refute the notion that I had undermined the church. They shrugged their shoulders and rolled their eyes. Some moved their lips, but it was apparent they had come to watch a hanging, not to be hanged. Finally, just when I thought my misery was never to end, the petty pastor raised his arm and with two little fingers pressed together slowly lowered his arm in an arc. From his huge mouth in a huge voice, he said, "I sever you from the body of Christ." For a moment, the room fell silent. The pastor, realizing the thin ice beneath his "excommunication," said, "I realize I don't have power to do this, but if you are as guilty as I believe you are, the Lord will certainly sever you from the body of Christ." Someone mumbled that they had other school business to conduct. I excused myself and walked numbly into the hall. There was a tap on my shoulder. It was the principal. "Don't forget to report to work tomorrow. You must clear up every item on the checkout list if you want your final paycheck," he said. I couldn't answer. Shocked surprise closed my throat. I stared stupidly at him. My voice returning, I wisecracked, "Excommunication doesn't get one out of work, I see." He did not smile. The principal repeated his command again. He was clearly not impressed with his pastor's power to consign one to hell and obviously even if I were on my way to hell, my principal was not going to let that interfere with more important matters. Other men in the hall, now suddenly out of the pastor's eyesight, found their voice, "Thank you for your ministry. My children really love you," and such good wishes. It was clear the doctrine of excommunication was a doctrine held even more weakly than tithing.

 I found my family waiting in the darkened sanctuary. My wife finally asked the dreaded question, "What did the pastor want?" I could tell from her tone that she shared my earlier optimistic hopes. She also thought the pastor would surely turn from vindictiveness. I was glad that the room was dimly lit, for if she could see my face, she would surely have known that I was not well. I said with a husky voice full of emotion, "The pastor had me meet with the board, and some other prominent men in the church for a trial. The pastor tried to excommunicate me." She thought I was making a joke. "Good old Mac, he's quite a joker." I didn't laugh nor could I laugh about that ridiculous night for a long time. The obvious humor I appreciate now, but only from a distance. You see, before I knew about inquisition, heresy trials, and martyrdom, but now I was uncomfortably close to feeling the pain of such things. Experience had altered my thinking forever with another lesson.

Incidentally, the pastor's church survived his poor administration, but the school's enrollment dropped by nearly 200 students. The school never recovered from firing me, but as I was told, "The pastor never believed a Christian school was necessary in the first place."

## Substituting Church Law for God's Law-Word

What did I learn from my first three years and my pseudo excommunication? Well, first, I learned that the perception of disloyalty to a pastor is a far greater sin than stealing or adultery. Before my experience, I knew that evangelical dispensational Christians did not believe they were bound to obey the commandments. They never tire of saying, "We are under grace, not law." Now I believed that the word of God or the law was not as important to them as the word of the strongest man in the church. In four more evangelical churches, I would see strong men (not usually the pastor) rule, in spite of openly breaking the commandments. Don't misunderstand. The Bible does indeed teach salvation by grace, but some modern churches have perverted that doctrine to mean that church members can continue in sin without change and still be certain that they are on the way to heaven. As a result, the practicing thief and adulterer, if thought to be loyal to the leader, is considered in grace. When man's law is substituted for God's, such perversion is the rule, not the exception. I am embarrassed to say that this painful lesson was taught to me several times.

## Robbing Widows in the Name of God

My next administrative job was as a principal of a Christian school run by a church in Havre de Grace, Maryland. I sold my trailer and with the money made a down payment on a very old house in a very old town called Perryville. Perryville, I came to learn, was famous for a hospital caring for insane soldiers. As I now think of it, that was the right place for me. Only I was in the Lord's army, but, in many regards, just as much out of touch with reality as the mentally broken soldiers of the United States Army. Christians who live according to their fancies instead of the law of God are truly insane.

My new pastor will serve as an illustration of just how insane such denial of reality can be. He had sold bonds to expand and pay for a church and school building too large for his church's income. When the church did not magically grow to be as full as his dreams (called prayers) demanded, he sold more bonds to pay for his previous bonds. As a matter of fact, he sold bonds to pay bonds for six successive separate issues of bonds. He called this walking by "faith." Sound familiar? After the sixth issue of bonds, he began to be hounded by the federal government for tax money withheld from the teachers' payroll.

The I.R.S. does not believe in walking by "faith." They won't walk without real money! My pastor hurriedly named a successor and ran to a new church in Michigan, where I fervently hope he did not continue to walk by "faith."

I had the retching experience of interviewing widows demanding payment for bonds. Painfully, I explained there was no money. The new pastor and I would try to get the church and school on a paying basis, but in the meantime, we could not meet the church's contractual obligations. After learning that their trust in the good pastor had been misplaced, the women would shuffle stoop-shouldered from my sight; the Bible verse, "Woe unto you, scribes and Pharisees, hypocrites! for ye devour widows' houses" (Matt. 23:14) would ring in my tormented mind.

The school was bankrupt. All the money was given to the government to keep the chain and seal from locking the doors forever. I was thrown on the charity of the church. My family was without income. Disgusted, I decided to leave Christian work. I interviewed with several Baltimore trucking companies with no success. "Overqualified," they said. "What's a guy with a master's degree recently completed at Johns Hopkins want with a freight sales job?" I tried to enter the Army as a chaplain. "Sorry, your graduate work suits you more for education than the ministry." The only door of opportunity was a principal's position at another Christian school in Maryland, just off the Washington, D.C. beltway. The Lord's will is not hard to find when you have only one choice.

By using a government loan program for poor families, I managed to qualify one of the poorest men in our church to buy my Perryville home. I still remember his wonder as we left the attorney's office. "Am I a homeowner now?" he asked in a hopeful tone. I could see the poor soul had not understood any of the proceeding. "Yes," I explained, "Although you put no money down, you did sign papers agreeing to pay $103 per month, gradually increasing with your future income. In thirty years, with the government subsidy, you will own the place free and clear. His eyes filled with tears of joy. "I'll have to call my mother. She won't believe this." I winced. What was a faithful right-wing, anti-socialistic Christian teacher like me doing in such a government scheme? Well, in Christian war as in other wars perhaps, one must use every means to victory. Soon a low church salary would crush me to my knees. I still had much to learn about service to the false god of lawlessness that pervades modern society. Sometimes I was told that my poverty was of my own making. As one of the preaching staff's wives aired her feelings, "Anyone in Christian work that has that many children is irresponsible." Her dislike of my normal-sized family was nearly universally shared by other "believers." Either I should have practiced birth control or left church work seemed to be the general consensus. In the Savannah church, my wife was widely pitied for allowing herself to be a "baby machine."

Experts record that 20 percent of church women are barren. The others have the usual 1.5 children. Of all the stubborn things, however, that I have accomplished—my graduate degrees, my financial success, my happy 37 years with the same faithful wife—none gives me more joy than the eight children who grace my table. There is no earthly honor or possession to be compared with a child. Sometimes an older person (man usually) would stop my wife and me outside the church and say, "You have such a happy, healthy family. I regret not having more children. I wish that we could have another chance, but it's too late. Do you know what I mean?" "No, I don't really know" was my unspoken thought. Outwardly, I would say, "Thank you, sir, for your encouragement. Many people are critical of a large family. I appreciate your kindness."

During those years, the notion that the world would be overpopulated was widely taught in every college. In the face of zero population growth, such nostrums have joined the Loch Ness Monster and similar fairy tales. We have global warming, nuclear waste, and homeless people to terrify pseudo-intellectuals at this writing. The myths of the church, when straying from Scripture, are small compared to the outrageous falsehoods of the secular university.

## False Doctrine Leads to Hard Service

There are many other horror stories I could recount here. I was jailed for handing out gospel tracts on the street in Greenville, South Carolina, and afterwards I was jailed in two other South Carolina cities. I was forbidden to preach on the street by my pastor in Savannah, Georgia. But I do not have space or inclination to bury the reader in such stories, no matter how amusing they may be in retrospect. Sufficient to say, I am very grateful for each of these experiences, for they have taught me that false doctrine can lead to hard service. The initial pain of my youthful impulsiveness has mellowed into an older man's reminiscences. Like a veteran soldier, the hardships are treasured memories because of the sweet victory that followed the battle. The Lord has bathed the wounds with success, which is both material and spiritual. That is why you may be reading this book, so you may benefit from my mistakes.

To sum up then, I have personally experienced:

1. Man's law in place of God's;
2. Bankrupt churches and schools;
3. Every school except the ones I have founded were financially in deep trouble;

4. Fraudulent bond sales (a businessman would have been labelled a felon).

## Success Breeds Guilt & Envy

My next lesson to learn was that success in some Christian circles breeds guilt and envy. My new school in Maryland was running a deficit. The enrollment was about 200 students. The school was wildly out of control. The halls were strewn with garbage, and on occasion, some of the students thought it great sport to defecate on the floor. Your eyes are not fooling you. Some did a number two on the floor.

The Lord blessed my efforts. By using a direct-mail advertising campaign, 1 was able to flood the school with nearly 100 new students per year. By careful administration, I was able to evade various church pressure groups and in five years, the school produced a surplus of over $100,000 per year. By any measure, this was a phenomenal success! I demanded, for the first time, a respectable salary of $32,000 per year.

For 1979, that was not as high as public school principals, but very high for a Christian school principal. In a tough game, I had emerged triumphant. My cup was full. Suddenly, the roof collapsed. The church was shrinking while my school had grown and that didn't look good for the pastor. While I received a raise, the church and school board passed over the pastor without a raise. Since he was not as strong a leader as my Savannah pastor, all seemed all right, but the men in the church soon witnessed a pastor brimming with envy. In the past, when the pastor's salary and benefits were rising, he played one church group against the other with skills only thirty years of pastoring can teach. I was soon to learn what harm an envious pastor can do. Now, I found my flanks not so well protected. To make a long story short, five and a half years of success ended with another sacking.

In a hurried effort to keep my family in housing, I became an automobile salesman until another school position could be found. The triumphant pastor hired his son from a small upper New York church to fill my job three weeks before the fall term was to open. (Both the son and the father lost their jobs in less than 18 months after I left.) After six months as an auto salesman, I accepted a post as principal for a another financially troubled Christian school in Wilson, North Carolina.

## More Success Produces Faster Sacking

The Wilson school was in debt to two powerful and wealthy men from the sponsoring church. The pastor was not a friend of Christian education. Before my arrival, he had already planned to close the facility. His own family had been reared in the public school, and he made no secret of his opinion that if the church was good, no Christian school was necessary. Providentially, his unbiblical notions were not shared by most of his church members, who had been taught the virtue of Christian education by sterner and wiser preachers before his tenure. The two financial "angels" backed up their faith in Christian education with a line of credit that totaled over $90,000 by the time they sat before me to hear my plan to resuscitate their ailing institution. To their delight and my new pastor's chagrin, I promised to put them in the black within a year and produce a surplus in two years. I demanded a salary of $34,000. Several of the board, as I later learned, resented the amount and my frank refusal to consider anything less. To shorten the account, the Lord blessed again, and in just two short years, a surplus approaching $100,000 was within sight.

The stage was set for this pilgrim to learn a lesson learned too often before. The board served notice that they would meet several times per year without my attendance. They also balked at giving me a raise. I quickly began looking for another school *before* I could be sacked again.

## A Golden Parachute to Save from Envy

As I sat brooding in my office on the eve of the day I was to fly to New England to interview for another position, I pondered, "Why must teaching success produce such anger?" The smiling face of one of my parents appeared at the door. He was a professional development officer (i.e., he raised money for nonprofit organizations). He was very happy to tell me that he had landed a new job with the Salvation Army. He waved in his hand a five-year contract. Curious, I asked, "Do you mind if I see that?" He didn't and I photostated the contract. I had a new plan. With just a few modifications, I stepped off the plane the next day in New England with a blank contract for my new school board to consider.

My prayer and plan was simple. If the Lord blessed me with success, I now knew anger by weak and failing Christians was sure to rear its ugly head. I presented my plan to salvage another failing school, but with a new twist at salary discussion time. The salary would be $39,000. If the contract was broken sooner than 5 years, one full year of severance pay had to be paid to me. The school was impressed with my track record, and they were needy and humble. (They always are at the beginning.) Inwardly, I breathed a prayer, "Lord, if this is your will, let it be with the contract. I am weary of moving. On second thought, Lord, I am content to do something else. Maybe this would be a nice way for you, Lord, to let me know it's OK to quit this Christian work?"

After I presented the contract, I excused myself from the board room saying, "If you have no other questions, I'll leave you to discuss your decision." I felt very certain that I would be delivered at last from Christian work. I almost skipped out of the school and up the hill to the board member's house, where I was spending the night. So confident was I that I went straight upstairs, took off my clothes, and was nearly asleep when the bad news came. The board was downstairs ready to welcome me to still another school.

Within two months, two pastors from the board saw me in private and bitterly told me that they despised my contract. They told me in hushed, holy voices that no pastor would name a figure and demand a contract as I had done. Proper procedure was simply to say, "If the Lord directs, I wish that my needs be met." Both of these men had voted for my contract, they said because the other "laymen" had been so enthusiastic about my supposed ability to rescue the school. Outwardly, I nodded my head, thanking them for their valuable counsel. Inwardly, I thought, envy will be even faster this time. I was right! The Lord had not taught the lesson in vain in Wilson. I had learned to expect treachery. The school was rescued from bankruptcy even faster, but this time to my surprise, the faculty rebelled. They did not like the contract either. Success came (to my surprise) in my church. My pastor became my friend and supporter. The school became my enemy, and the church became my friend, just when I thought I could foresee all things!

## Churchmen Fail to Honor Own Written Word

In time, as I prophesied to my new pastor friend (in two years), the board was rallying to fire me; but this time I did not rush for another position. I waited to see what they would do with the contract. I predicted to my new friend, my pastor, that the board would refuse to pay the year's pay. "Why?" he asked in amazement. I replied, "Because they are full of guilt over their incompetence and in a rage of envy."

This time I did see the future only too clearly. I know it may be a surprise to many Christians that churches often do not pay their bills and that a board of pastors and Christian laymen would try to break a written contract; but that is the rule, not the exception, according to this pilgrim's experience. They offered to pay nothing, then to pay a part, and then $22,000 and finally— after I hired a Harvard attorney—they paid the full year, withholding my vacation pay. After an additional three years of threats and just before the trial date, they offered to pay half the vacation pay. The insurance company offered to pay the remainder, so I settled, rather than air these details in court. Shocking to report, to this day they have refused to pay my wife's vacation pay on the flimsy excuse that she quit and left her job just because her husband had been fired.

The Harvard attorney had far more honor than the board members. He labored without any pay for over three years, drawing up paper after paper to help me sell my house without charging a dime. He took only a small part of the vacation settlement for part of his expenses.

Sad to say, the pastors I have known have fully earned their miserable poverty, failing churches, failing health and failing homes. Men calling themselves "servants of God" refused to honor their written word. Remarkable to report, to this day, they assure all who will listen that I am of the devil, because I threatened to sue. These matters rest in the hands of the Lord. I leave the resolution to my Savior.

What were the lessons? I decided that if teaching is to be anything different, a new plan and vision is needed. I prayed for wisdom.

Today in the spring of 1996 with six schools full of happy children with parents clamoring to enroll their precious students, I know now that those prayers cast into the sky over that New England pond were heard and answered beyond my fondest hope. I cried out to the Lord for wisdom from the cancerous stupidity that eats at many schools—public, private, and even Christian. Always merciful and generous when the prayer for wisdom is made, the Lord not only rescued me, but you, dear reader, as well, if only you will give Him your attention.

# CHAPTER V
# My Road to Freedom

My son, Bart, secured the safety chains of the trailer and I slid behind the wheel of the crowded 1979 Ford wagon. As the interstate cleared of icy conditions, I relaxed and considered my plan. I had the $39,000 of severance pay and another $51,000 equity from the sale of my home in New Hampshire and another former home in Maryland. My mother had generously offered to give me free rent until I could find another position. Her Florida home was irresistible after New Hampshire. What skills did I have? Well, a specialist in rescuing mismanaged schools or an overeducated car salesman seemed to be the sum. Perhaps this time I could buy the school. That is a great idea. These churchmen were desperate enough to sign a contract. Perhaps I could talk them out of a whole school. Using my direct-mail techniques, I could flood the school with new students and survive that inevitable moment when their churches would withdraw their students. Thereby, I could have a Christian school free from the smothering incompetence of a church. The next $100,000 surplus I earned would be mine. The school property would be laid up for my children. Why not? My family deserved an inheritance, as the Scripture verse, "A good man leaveth an inheritance to his children's children," (Prov. 13:22) came to mind.

We stopped in Fairfax, Virginia, to visit some former teaching associates. They were now on the faculty of a school administered by a conservative Presbyterian. The school was wholly owned by an individual. I studied the school. Could this be the model for me? I asked the owner if he knew of a school similar to his that I could buy? Being a very kind and gracious man, he tried very hard to find such a school but without success. While we were riding in his car, however, we chanced by a daycare center. He followed my gaze toward the center and remarked, "Now, there's an idea." "What's that?" I asked. "Well, he added, "a man could locate several small schools similar to those as feeders to a larger central school." The subject of the conversation changed, but my mind raced toward a plan.

### Daycare as a Seed Bed

A preschool seemed obvious as the way to begin a school. Instead of beginning at K-5 or first grade, why not begin where the market was begging for vendors—daycare. It was suddenly plain. Why had I not seen this before?

Arriving in Bonita Springs, Florida, I started searching for property and a contractor. The risks were very great. After all, I was a fifty-year-old man with a large family. What if I failed? Fainthearted, I applied for a position with another school, but the door was closed. The New Hampshire school board persuaded my recommending agency that I was "unfit" since I had threatened to sue them. This only strengthened my resolve to press toward independence and the promise of freedom. There was no way but forward. The will of the Lord is very plain when only one option is available.

My mother made good her promise of free rent, but her second marriage, after my father's death, was not going as well as she had hoped. Then she was stricken with stomach cancer. I had even less time and capital than I had planned to start a school and care for my family. Renting a home for a family of eight, if possible to find such a home, was not within my budget. I packed up my family, and we moved into a campground near Naples. We lived there for seven months. I visited bank after bank, seeking a mortgage for a house and school. To my chagrin, bankers were not impressed with educational credentials; they regarded ministers as poor business risks (I certainly couldn't argue with that!). They hinted that my plan called for long hours. Could I work that hard? It seemed they thought that teachers and ministers were lazy (I couldn't argue about that!). They kept asking for proof that I could make a profit. It seemed that they thought ministers were insipid Marxists (I very certainly couldn't argue with that). I gathered profit-and-loss sheets, and letters of testimony stating that I could and had always made a profit. I had a pile of such letters.

Finally, by accident, or more properly, the Lord's design, I chanced on a city bank executive who was taking a local manager's place for a summer vacation. At last, face to face with a decision-maker, I won a construction loan for the school. We opened our first school on February 3,1986 with 24 students. In a brief three months, it crossed into the black. The Lord had, at last, given me freedom.

I still remember that April morning when the tyranny of the profit and loss statement spelled freedom to my eager eyes. I floated out the side door to the playground and flopped down on one of the low picnic tables. The warm winter Florida sun bathed me as I listened to the happy shrieks of the children at play. No more school boards, no more church boards, no more assurances of their insincere praise; I was free! Thank God, free at last! I burst out laughing. I recognized that I was quoting

Martin Luther King. Well, I wasn't black, but I had known the chains of slavery.

## The Idiot Provider

I still had one surprise, however, when I showed my balance sheet to the bank: "Sorry, but we cannot give you a mortgage for a house. Yes, you are making money, but a new business must have at least two years' experience." Shocked, I had to tell my wife that two years of campground life may be in prospect. She did not cry this time. As a matter of fact, over the brutal years of grinding poverty, she had cracked only once. She was true to her stoic Scotch heritage. We lived in a New Hampshire campground from June 1983, until the first week of December waiting for a house to be built. Delay after delay kept us in the campground until the pipes froze, and the season's first snow started to fall. Our children, ever happy to live in the worst of conditions, rose laughing and dancing about welcoming the snow, like pagan wood nymphs. As I laughed to watch them sticking out their tongues to catch the flakes of snow and whirling about with outstretched arms, I caught the sight of Patricia (Wallace) McIntyre. Down dropped the curtain of the usual adamant self-control. Her usual patience gave way to despair as she muttered, "I can't take it anymore," and then just as quickly caught herself. In a flash, I felt ashamed to be the poor provider that I was. She deserved better!

Now with the prospect of two more years of camping, Florida's rainy season came pouring down on our trailer's tin roof. Outside, the boys moved their tent onto wood pallets in a vain attempt to escape the dampness. But with the school, we had lots of money. I bought a lot across the street from the school for cash and began to build a house for cash. I had reserved a fund as extra capital. It was a dangerous business practice to spend all my cash, but what was another risk? My sons built the house in only 58 days. They labored up to 12 hours per day. They too had some Scotch in their blood.

## Raised from the Dunghill

July 4, 1986 found us still not in our house but very close. Worried about my wife, I booked a weekend at the Ritz Carlton Hotel on Vanderbilt Beach. We arrived at the hotel 3:00 p.m. on the dot, hoping no one would notice that campground bums were invading the place. In front of us, a very snooty couple listened to the clerk apologize that their room was not ready yet, but the clerk did have a substitute room available with only one king-sized bed instead of two separate beds. The snooty wife went off into a rage, "Certainly not!" I felt sorry for the clerk.

Ducking around the couple, I said, "My wife and I are friendly enough for one bed." The snooty woman glared, and my wife blushed. The clerk forced back a smile and pushed a key over the counter. With perky aplomb, she explained that we would be upgraded at no extra charge to the club floor. The extra key would allow us exclusive use of the elevator to reach our outrageously expensive luxury at no additional charge. With deep satisfaction, we sat on our private balcony overlooking the gulf, and with a warm hug, I quoted to my wife, "He hath raised us from the dunghill and made us to sit with princes" (I Sam. 2:8).

## More Success

We opened our second school in Golden Gate on May 2, 1988 with 48 students enrolled and 4 teachers with 2 aides. One year later, we had 153 students enrolled with 8 teachers and 2 aides and a waiting list of 15. This school broke even from the first day.

The third Grace Community School, located in Naples Park, was under construction by April 1988. It opened its doors on September 12,1988 with 43 students enrolled and 2 teachers with 3 aides. This school broke even the first day also. It soon had 114 students and 7 teachers with 4 aides.

This outstanding success is particularly significant in view of the fact that Collier County at the time had only 1,750 kindergarten children entering its system each year. The total number of single-family homes was only about 30,000, if we include the entire trading area of Naples. What we have convincingly demonstrated is that this enterprise is reproducible in Naples, which is a very weak market. The chances are the reader's market is much larger than Naples. Imagine how much better you can do in your market!

## CHAPTER VI
# Why My Plan Works

### Customer is Sovereign

Why does my plan produce a profit while others cannot? Very simply put, the business that succeeds best serves the customer best. The customer is the sovereign of the marketplace. Serve that king and good things happen. Cross the customer/king and bad things happen. Public schools serve the politician first, not the customer first. Church schools serve the church first, not the customer. Both public and Christian schools refuse to live and die for profit. Instead, they speak in great swelling, lofty tones of service to God in the case of the church, or service to mankind in the case of the government. As a consequence, they serve poorly all concerned. It will be my sad duty one day to accuse them before the throne of God.

However, there are limits to the customer's sovereignty. If we were to provide just what the customer wants in a strict bowing to the sovereignty of the customer, we should throw out all Bible instruction. Instead, we assure the parent that we will not push a particular church or a controversial Bible doctrine. You see, we believe the customer should get what she wants up to a point, but ultimately, we serve another master. Does that seem strange? Well, doesn't the public school serve a purpose other than the parent? Also, doesn't the church school? Also doesn't the humanistic school? A careful examination will reveal that, of all schools, ours serve the customer best, because we do not receive tax money, church money, United Fund money, or any funding other than the customer's. As a result, our product must please the customer or we die. We have no alternate money source to corrupt our system. We do, however, teach the Bible. We ultimately serve the Lord.

In my system, the customer pays a competitive tuition for a product he is willing to buy. The public system has a product that more and more will not accept, even when it seems free! The church has a product too often, at least in the customer's view, only slightly better than the public school.

In my system, the teacher is the owner. The teacher lies down to sleep and awakes with one thought in mind—how to serve the parent better than his competitors. Why? Because he wants a profit for his family. Is that bad? Well, listen to the Apostle Paul, "I press toward the mark the prize of the high calling in Christ Jesus; henceforth, there is laid up for me a crown [reward]" (Phil. 3:4). If reward was good enough to make Paul run, it is good enough for me. Or consider Matt. 6:33, "Seek ye first the kingdom of God… and all of these things shall be added unto you." What things? Matt. 6:33 in context is referring to Solomon's wealth. In other words, obey as did Solomon and enjoy earthly treasure as did Solomon. The verses are far too numerous to list here but suffice to point out that labor for a reward is not unholy when pursued to the glory of God. Those who deny incentive for reward are the ungodly among us. As a matter of fact, chief among the ungodly who scoff at reward are communists and their brother socialists. We all know, since Russia and her satellites have collapsed, how poorly systems work without the profit motive. Schools and churches can hope for no better fate as long as they refuse to kneel before the law-word of God.

## Advertising Pays Off

In the public system, advertising is usually not used except as a public relations gimmick. For example, in my county, it is popular to have a bumper sticker saying, "I have an honor student at name of public school." Considering the depressed levels of scholarship at public schools, I am not sure what the sticker signifies.

Private schools typically regard advertising as a stigma of being second-rate. Reverse snobbery then prevents extensive and open use of advertising by private schools.

My system, on the other hand, will inspire the owner/ teacher to overcome his anti-advertising mentality. Profit motive will, most likely, even impel the teacher/owner to find many noble reasons to advertise, such as public service, or improving the climate of education through healthy competition, or best of all, to win children to Christ. Marvelous thing about my system—it brings out the noble, selfless spirit in parents.

## Parental Sovereignty

Our society has produced situations which require both parents to absent themselves from the home in order to earn a decent living. Religious zealots will argue that mother should stay home under all circumstances. For example, I have had my advertisement for those interested in working in or owning a private daycare/school rejected by "churchy" publications on the basis that "daycare just does not fit our philosophy."

On another occasion, a woman telephoned me long distance from Texas to complain about my school. It seemed some women in her Presbyterian church were going to meet and discuss starting a church school using a daycare as a building platform. She called to ask how I could justify enticing women to leave their children to work outside the home. I tried to explain that my parents are single for various reasons, in addition to economic reasons. There is divorce and similar situations. As Christians, we should be ready to evangelize children from such homes. Repeatedly, she kept saying, "Yes, but how can you provide your service without tempting mothers to work?" The phone connection was very poor. I offered to call back. She said, "It won't do any good; the mobile phone in this limousine is always full of static." Amazingly, I thought how can this woman ever really feel and understand the plight of a mother who must work?

Let us admit that the McIntyre educational system is very successful. As a result, we draw children into our school from homes where the mother does not really have to work. Yes, we do draw such children! But is that a reason to turn our back on mothers who must work? Should we withhold the gospel from children of poor or broken homes? We choose to serve and obey the Lord by meeting the needs of the working mother and her needy children.

### Customer Pays a Competitive Tuition

The tender conscience of the Christian should consider that the working mother can get child care from many, many non-Christian sources. The rate is set by the marketplace. Several large national chains are traded on public stock exchanges. We are not providing services that cannot be purchased at a price, but we may be providing the only Christian alternative at a fair competitive tuition. The question best framed then is, "Shouldn't we meet the anti-Christian product and rate? Shouldn't we compete for the heart and soul of that child?"

Let us also recognize that the customer sometimes does not want a Christian daycare/school. The Bible component is looked on as a negative by many parents.

## Who Has the Need for Our Service?

All of our customers, both Christian and non-Christian alike, believe they need to buy our service. We do not force our service on anyone. The customer enters voluntarily into our system, choosing our service from among all competing services.

## What the Market Really Wants

Let us consider what the school customer really wants. My system offers safe care from 7 a.m. to 6 p.m. on a year-round basis with only the normal ten paid holidays. That is what the working mother wants. She does not want only 180 school days per year and supervision for only 5 to 6 hours per day.

We offer genuine academic subjects even to children age two. Our average K-5 graduates score on national standardized tests at the second-grade level. Bright children often read at the fifth-grade level. That is a product a mother wants, not the child who watches television all day. Do not misunderstand; we provide plenty of play time, but unlimited play can be boring. We are experts at making school "fun." A proper mixture of work and play makes a life worthwhile and "fun" for both adult and child. Too much of either one goes against the grain. Just allow a tractor, an electric lineman, a plumber, or any kind of work activity come in view of a playground. What happens? All of the toys suddenly lose their charm. The children press against the fence yelling endless questions, "What are you doing? Why?" etc. When you work at home, are not your children forever under foot? Meaningful work is fun! The child wants meaningful activity, and the mother wants education with activity for her child.

## Teacher Is the Owner of the School

The teacher is in control of his capital. Ownership is central to forecast the direction that any organization will follow. When the government owns the school, very predictable results follow. The student will be taught that government is the proper place to go to solve his problems. Ask any American product of the public system his solution to nearly any problem, and his answer will nearly always contain this premise, "The government should do something about that." The knee-jerk reaction to pollution, energy shortage, homeless people, population control, low-cost housing, gay rights, civil rights, etc. (the problem varies, but the solution seldom does), "There ought to be a law or a government program" is the sure and certain response of the brainwashed public school product. Those who wish to manipulate America into more socialism need only dream up or drum up or point out real or imaginary problems. Child abuse, spouse abuse, you name it—and the inveterate response of the semi-educated American will be less private property, more public property or control, or both.

More growth, faster growth, and runaway growth of big government is the inevitable trend of a society when schools are owned and controlled by government. The one to whom you turn for the ultimate answer to your problems is your god. Our children have been taught to turn to government as the ultimate answer to all their problems. In other words, they have been taught to worship the government.

## The Perverted Church vs. the Word of God

If the church controls the school, the direction of society is equally predictable. The child will be taught that the church is the ultimate good and perfect answer for most problems. A society that educates its young in church schools will surely bend the knee to the church by and by. Napoleon unwittingly ensured that result when the young of France were allowed to be taught in church schools. A new generation arises more quickly than old men realize. The maxim "the hand that rocks the cradle rules the world," is true beyond dispute.

Under my system, the teacher controls his own property. The teacher controls his own curriculum. The teacher controls his relationship with the children and parents. That is an advantage in every way! My system is the ultimate decentralization except perhaps for a total home school system (not a bad system either). The parent replaces the state, church, and the all-powerful central educational agency for directing the education of the child. The teacher cannot resist the desires of the parent when the parent has many competing schools, all dependent upon his tuition money. Do most parents want reading, math, and science more than social engineering? We all know the answer to that question. Under which system would most parents get what they want? Do not most parents want the values of the Ten Commandments taught?

## The More Central the Control, the More Unlimited the Evil

The genius of capitalism is decentralization vs. communistic centralized totalitarian government. An important lesson of history is that, given the evil in man, the more central the control, the more unlimited the evil. Limited power has always been the best solution to most problems. Good schools check and balance bad schools, just as bad men are checked and balanced by good men, provided that good men are free to own and control private property. Where did that idea come from? "Thou shalt not steal" and "Thou shalt not covet" (Exodus 20)—two of the Decalogue of God's law demand private property. An evil government teaches that public land for "all the people" is always best. An evil church teaches that the church should sanctify the land by its ownership. "Give it to God," they say. God's word, on the other hand, teaches, "A good man layeth up for his children's children."

Private property owned by families is the Bible's model of control. Is it any wonder that, as a general rule, the larger and more powerful the government or church, the lower esteem in which the law of God is held? This educator prays for the day when most education will be controlled by families or small decentralized churches, or individual Christian educators subject to the law of God. We can never have a perfect school system, because we do not have perfect men. We at least should have a decentralized system. In an imperfect world of imperfect men, a decentralized economy, decentralized government, and a decentralized school system are the best of all possible worlds.

### How to Keep Schools Decentralized

It does not take much faith to believe that if a teacher's salary is directly dependent on pleasing his client, the school will serve the client. Likewise, it is easy to believe that if a teacher's pension is independently based on private investment, the sticky, incompetent hands of the government will not rob or influence the teacher. Most of all, I am sure that if the school building is to be an inheritance for the teacher's children, the building will be lovingly maintained, free from graffiti, and a credit to the aesthetics of the community. I am also certain that advertising should be part of the teacher's sales tools. A free market produces a surplus of quality goods and services, which makes advertising a must for those who serve a free market. Only a closed market can long survive without salesmanship. It is the Christian way and should also be the American way.

### Cost-Cutting is Rewarded

My system produces a profit. Because we are all students of teachers who deprecate profit, did not know how to make a profit, and are apt to regard profit as a crime, we need to justify earning money. Surprisingly, schools not operated for a profit are the most expensive. America's public schools spend more per pupil than any other advanced country for the worst results of any advanced country. New Hampshire, for example, spends less than most states per pupil, but still has the highest average test scores in the entire nation. The taxpayer is victimized under the government nonprofit system. Remember that the secret goal of all government is to get more people on the payroll, not to improve the service. Bungling inefficiencies are welcome, because such failure stimulates hiring more people to correct the problem. The problem is this: those trained by the government have been educated in the wrong direction. They cannot believe government itself to be a bad idea; they envy and despise the profit-making, enterprising schools. Someone has substituted black for white and white for black!

When a private school makes a profit, the parent is not victimized but served. The school's profit cannot long be kept a secret. Competitors will enter the market and keep on entering until the margin of profit is down to the place where new competitors see the profit as too small for competitive risk. A high profit then ensures that the supply of schools will increase. A high profit also cushions the school against the risk of recession and unexpected rise in costs. A high profit means that the best teachers will seek the private sector for its higher salaries. In short, for the same reasons that capitalism is superior to all other systems, profit, if not gained by fraud, rewards all concerned.

## Growth of the School is More Rapid

Luke 14:29-30 reads, "Lest haply after he hath laid the foundation and is not able to finish it. All that behold it begin to mock him, saying, 'This man began to build and was not able to finish.'" These verses describe the wisdom of advance planning. Our school plan must be one that has the most promise for victory. Why follow the plan of the public school? Has that system produced what we want? Likewise, is the Christian church school likely to grow as rapidly and prosper as well as a school run for profit? Now is the time to sit down and count the cost. We will well deserve the mocking derision of our enemies if we fail to learn from the defeat of others. The problems of other schools, referred to in this book, are advantages to anyone who builds by my plan. If public, private, and Christian schools refuse or cannot grow as intelligent, self-interested enterprises, that is so much the better for us. The next chapter will outline a few of the secrets of my success, which can make your enterprise intelligent and rewarding.

# Photos

*Grace Community School buildings prominently feature our name, the whale logo, and Matt. 12:40.*

*They might have some variations, but our buildings are unmistakably Grace Community Schools.*

*Attractive landscaping ("curb appeal") is an important part of Grace Community School brand Image.*

*The whale, referring to Matt. 12:40, is taught to the children as a sign of the prophet Jonas and the resurrection of Christ. Our buildings include a distinctive whale weathervane on top.*

*Grace Community School provides free before and after school transportation to and from local public schools so older students can receive Bible instruction. Our pickup vans are wrapped with school logo, website, and other branding elements.*

*Branding and marketing is crucial for the success of the Christian school. We take every opportunity to promote our services and thereby promote Christ.*

*We put the whale logo everywhere.*

*"Gracie the Whale" is our school mascot and a key part of school branding. She makes appearances at graduation and Christmas shows and special events throughout the year.*

*A highlight of our musical performances for parents is the moment Gracie the Whale comes onstage.*

*Grace Community School has its own school song complete with music video (also featuring Gracie the Whale). As of early 2021 the YouTube video had more than 1.1 million views.*

*At the end of each school year, our kids put on a musical dance performance for parents and grandparents culminating in a preschool and kindergarten graduation.*

*Kindergarten graduates with their diplomas in caps and gowns.*

*Graduates shake the principal's hand and take their diplomas during the kindergarten graduation ceremony.*

*Our graduation programs include a public performance of reading ability. This is a powerful testimony of the success of our phonics reading curriculum.*

*By using the daycare years to teach reading, the typical student has a two-year advantage. Children take home their Grace Community School reading books to show their parents how they have progressed.*

*Reading Circles are one on one and small group phonics instructional periods that occur throughout the day.*

*Grace Community School's College Can Begin at 2 Curriculum includes teacher and student phonic instructional books, everything the teacher needs to teach children as young as two years of age how to read.*

*Math Circles are also a part of the curriculum. As with Reading Circles, students take home certificates showing their progress as they advance through levels of ability.*

*Grace Community School kindergarten students hard at work.*

*Grace Community School students working on an art project.*

*All classroom learning activities, drill times, worksheets, and art projects work together with each week's theme to make learning enjoyable for both students and teachers.*

*Bible Time, done twice a day, includes pledges to the Bible, Christian flag, and American flag.*

*Children from ages two years and up learn the foundational Bible stories along with the 23$^{rd}$ Psalm, Lord's Prayer, and the Ten Commandments with illustrations.*

*Children view Grace Community School as much more than a school or daycare. It is a second home to them, and their teachers and the management family that run each location are family.*

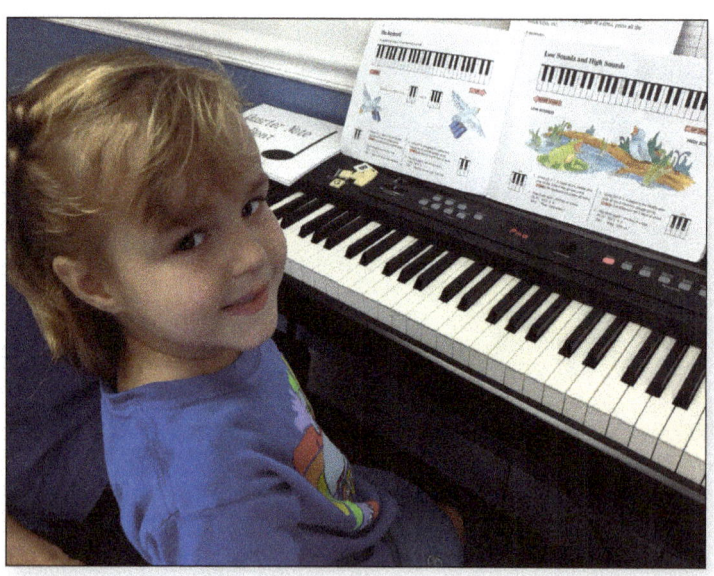

*Music lessons, including practice with instruments and music theory, are available to Grace Community School students.*

*Grace Community School locations also have a dance program.*

*Karate lessons help to install self-discipline and are another way for students to get physical exercise.*

*Grace Community School locations have excellent outdoor play areas. In addition to allowing for physical education, these are tremendous selling points for parents.*

*A Grace Community School infant room. Children are accepted as young as six weeks old.*

*A Grace Community School prekindergarten classroom.*

*A McIntyre family photo from 2019. Pastor McIntyre and wife Patricia have more than seventy children, grandchildren, and great-grandchildren. They have been married more than 60 years.*

*Rev. and Mrs. McIntyre celebrating the 35<sup>th</sup> anniversary of Grace Community School in February 2021.*

CHAPTER VII
# The Secrets of Success

### Meet a Growing Need: Working Mothers

Every politician from the President of the United States down to the dog catcher is howling about the need for child care. They are correct about the need. The biggest reward in such a market is to the teacher/entrepreneur who best meets the customers' need. Most schools—public, private, and church related—are tied to old forms developed before World War II, when most mothers stayed home, while the husband earned the bread. Begrudgingly, some schools have added extended care, but these are very weak band-aid solutions that my system conquers. Why? Because America's parents are waking up to many school problems. For example, low reading, low math, poor discipline and most painful, limited service, (the school is open only 180 days out of a 365-day year.) Every time the parent turns around, she must find a sitter for a school holiday. In my area, the public schools added something new, "Teacher Stress Day." I believe the school should relieve the parents of stress.

The stream of interruptions to the care provided by the public schools is astonishing. All the free enterprise teacher needs to do is provide reliable warehousing to best the competition. But if, in addition, the free enterprise school adds an academic program that solves or even tends to solve these other problems, the wealth of the market will pour into its lap. This is not just a theory. My system really does solve all and is described step by step in our operational manual.

## What About Depression?

What if a depression were to hit the nation? A depression is always a terrible thing for most businesses to face. All businesses, however, do not suffer during a business turndown. For example, used car parts and secondhand automobile businesses go up. In other words, some businesses are counter-cyclical. The used car parts businessman smiles when the depression comes and frowns when things are booming. What about daycare/preschools? Do more mothers enter or leave the marketplace during a depression? About 50 percent stay at home in normal times, but when things get rough, the husband has to get a lower paid job and his salary sags. The family must have an extra paycheck to meet the installment debt and mortgage on the house. Isn't that a comfort to the daycare/preschool? You bet. Wait, there's more. What happens when things are booming? Don't young families tend to buy too big a house, too nice a car, too plush furniture, too fancy appliances, too elegant vacations, etc. Yes, it is a fact of life. When (note when, not if) the young couple overextend themselves, drawn along by the siren song of endless prosperity, will Mother go to work sooner in order to keep up with the Joneses? You don't have to tune in tomorrow or even wait for the news at eleven o'clock to know the answer to that.

The free enterprise Christian teacher can smile in all seasons. Up, down, flat or sideways, you will be certain to have clients. The demand for daycare is what economists call "inelastic." It is what laymen call, "The best of all commercial worlds."

## Providing Good Moral Environment

When an investor considers my school, there is usually an inbred skepticism about the religious component of the program. The folk wisdom around the countryside is that the school must be stripped of all moral religious baggage to be really attractive to the most people. Most Christians have unwittingly created and nurtured this widespread belief. Many Christian schools, fired by well-meaning zeal, have tried to pound religion down the throats of all in sight. As a direct consequence, Christian educators have made themselves unwelcome, not only at the local beer parlor, but in polite company as well. What is surprising is this: both the boys at the beer parlor and polite company do not mind "some" religion for children. It's only the overzealous who frightens them. Solution? Just get the Scripture verses out of their faces, stop buttonholing them every time they cross your path, stop the constant sentimental invitations, and use the opportunities at hand. Tone it down! When they note the wonderful improvement in their children, your testimony will be irresistible. They will come to you with questions, if you are wise and cautious in your conversation. If you don't pluck green fruit, as the country preacher says, your school will be more attractive to more people than the cold, sterile, humanistic school. We need more than a confession of faith to succeed. Think about it. I seldom meet a parent who doesn't want his child to learn and obey God's law.

## Providing Masculine Leadership

Many, if not most, of the children in the typical preschool will come from homes without masculine leadership. This has an effect on sex-role development. As a college text for teachers states, "A sizable body of research suggests that fathers are particularly important in their children's sex-role development. One reason is that fathers care much more about sex typing than mothers do. . . . Cross-sex play tends to upset men, especially with regard to their sons." (Maccoby, 1980) as cited by Human Development, Papolia & Olds, 3rd ed., McGraw-Hill, NY, p. 215.

Given this fact, boys in particular will suffer in female-headed homes; therefore, the best preschool will fill this void with male leadership. In my system, a male must lead the morning and afternoon pledges and Bible lesson. It is important that the child experience at least one male in his life, who is a Godly role model. Little boys learn how to please girls by watching Mother react to Father. Since the boy's heart is toward Mother (if you doubt this, remind yourself whom the athlete says "hello" to when the TV camera gives him an opportunity. Isn't it 99 percent of the time, "Hi, Mom"?), the child will learn and imitate what his mother teaches him about men. The mother makes the man, not the father the son.

The reverse is true for girls. Little girls learn how to please boys by watching Daddy's reaction to Mother. Since the daughter's heart is centered on Daddy, she will learn from Dad, not Mother, how to be a woman. Given the truth of this, it becomes even more critical to have both sexes represented in the teaching staff of the school.

Armed with this information, ask yourself how to make your daughter regard "brains" as just as important as her "looks." Simple, the father must praise the mother more for her "brains" and less for her "looks." Conversely, if we wish our boys to be less enamored with "jocks" and more interested in scholarship, the mother must praise the father more for his "scholarship" and less for his "muscles." If both parents' role-play in this manner until it becomes second nature, they can influence their child's sex-role identity, at least the theory directs. To quote again from the same text, "If the father is so important to his children's sex-role development, what happens to those children who grow up in mother-headed, single-parent homes? Some children, especially those who are 5 or younger, when their fathers leave or die, seem to suffer either by becoming rigidly sex-typed or by taking on behaviors associated with the other sex to an inappropriate degree." (Hetherington, Cox & Cox, 1975 p. 216)

Men are needed, men are wanted, and men must be in a quality preschool. Men, however, are subject to special regulations laid out in our operational manual that protect them from child abuse accusations.

## Genuine Reading Instead of Phony Reading Readiness

It is a popular mistake to confuse reading readiness with genuine reading instruction. Every preschool in America seems to boast about their superior education program. By superior, they certainly do not mean reading; because every graduate school, to this doctor of education's knowledge, teaches to the prospective teacher that reading should not be taught to children in a preschool. I have received angry letters from educators who were triggered into rage just by the slogan that appears in our advertising, "College Can Begin at Two." It is an article of humanistic religion that young children should not be taught to read, but it is all right to spend hours talking about shapes, sizes, colors, and other abstract things that really do not need to be taught in the preschool.

The real reason, I suspect, that the American preschool or early childhood educator spends so much time on the difference between a triangle and a square and a square and a parallelogram and equally wearying tedium is that they have hours to waste that could be better spent teaching children symbols such as A, E, I, O, U. Since a child already knows how to use the vowels, it is a simple matter to transfer his hearing knowledge to symbolic knowledge set down on a written page. If a child can hear and understand language, he can read and understand language alphabetically set down on a page. There is no barrier except the teacher's self-imposed prison cell of discredited philosophy.

Some public school teachers have boasted to me that our Grace Community graduates, after entering fourth grade in the public school, do not have much of an advantage over public school children who have not received preschool reading instruction. This seems to prove to them that preschool reading instruction is a waste of time. Oddly, none of them seem to come to the more obvious conclusion that public schools hold back reading in a lock-step fashion, so the child who is already reading must wait until his classmates catch up. In other words, public school has squandered the head start by not building on the foundation already laid. For this reason, we tell parents who must transfer their children from our preschool to a public school, that it is crucial to take the child to the library and get him to constantly read ahead of his contemporaries.

Any skill not regularly practiced gradually wanes. For example, when my mother was in the third grade, she was able to read the American newspapers and translate them into Italian for her parents. But when she was in her twenties, she was no longer speaking and reading Italian daily. She was barely able to carry on a conversation in Italian. This doesn't mean, of course, that time invested in learning a skill is a complete loss, since the discipline of character to acquire any skill is readily transferable to every area of life. If your child is reading at the fifth-grade level by his sixth birthday, he will have a facility of language and an academic character that cannot be taken from him and more importantly, a positive attitude toward abstract learning, instead of the often negative attitude children pick up in inferior schools.

## Children Reading at 3 or 4 Make Very Satisfied Clients

Another great advantage to teaching reading instead of shapes, colors, and sizes is the public relations value of a child who can read. One of our parents told us about a dinner at an exclusive restaurant, where a tuxedo-attired waiter approached their table with a blackboard in his hand, listing the various French wines for the customer's selection. Before the waiter could speak, the child began to phonetically read the names of the wines. Since the child was only three or four years old, the waiter was astonished; and of course, the parents were very proud, because the waiter felt that the child had to be a genius. Of course, the waiter heard no argument about that. When the parents returned to Grace Community, they excitedly told the story of how they had learned the difference between genuine reading and "reading readiness."

On another occasion a four-year-old boy transferred from our preschool to another. The mother told the new preschool teacher not to embarrass her child by getting him to recite color recognition, because the boy was color blind. When the first week was over, the teacher told the mother that she was quite mistaken, because the child could see colors perfectly. The mother said, "No, you are mistaken. The boy is color blind."

The teacher argued, "Well, when I say, 'Color the sky blue,' he accurately picks up the blue crayon, and when I say, 'Make the leaves green,' he always picks up the correct crayon."

The mother smiled indulgently and said, "That is easy to explain. He is reading the colors written on the crayon." The jaw of the teacher dropped slack, and she stammered, "Can he read?"

The mother called the child to her, selected a printed page at random, and asked the child to read. The child read fluently with no hesitation.

At Grace Community, we have many such stories, because we live in a society that superstitiously refuses to teach children to read at an early age. It is our prayer that some day this superstition will vanish from our land. As a school owner, using our manual, you will do your part.

### Paraprofessional Teachers

If you use a large law firm, you are familiar with paraprofessional legal aides. These are people who do legal work under the supervision of a licensed practitioner. The same is true of medical facilities, engineering firms, and other professional associations. It is only in education that every classroom has to have a fully licensed practitioner. For this reason, the cost of education is higher than necessary to the parent, and the salary to the licensed practitioner is lower than in other professionals, such as engineers, lawyers, doctors, etc. In our operational manual, we will show you how to arrange your school so that you can use paraprofessionals in various specialties to multiply the productivity of the licensed teacher. This is an obvious innovation that has to be made in education if the cost of education is to be brought under control. Surprisingly, paraprofessionals boost the learning effectiveness of the school. Greater numbers of teachers or licensed practitioners do not equal greater education. Instead, because the salary for licensed teachers is low, the caliber of the people seeking these positions sinks lower and lower. In our school, one four-year degree or Masters-degree teacher is easily able to supervise the education of more than 100 students. The technology to do so is set forth in our manual. Why this obvious change has not been made years ago in our public school system has its roots in the economic blindness that permeates American education.

## The Secret of Wealth Creation

It is tempting to say that much of America has forgotten the economic fundamentals of capitalism. Forgotten is not the correct term, however, because I believe capitalism was never really taught in America. This economic blindness has deeper roots than mere academics; it is spiritual as well. The entrepreneur or capitalist creates wealth. The entrepreneur can make one plus one equal six and not two. The difference between two and six is the creative skill of the entrepreneur. This is capitalism. As Christ multiplied the loaves and fishes, so can the capitalist multiply goods under his gifted hands. The entrepreneur takes land, tools, labor, and money and uses them in a highly intelligent and creative fashion that is in harmony so that they produce more than when in a disharmonious and unorganized relationship to each other. The American Indian trod over all the natural resources of America for hundreds of years but was not able to adequately support himself. The Calvinist Christian imbued with the Protestant work ethic produced the most productive nation the world has ever known. Fidelity to the covenant of God produces wealth, as the word of God instructs, "But thou shalt remember the Lord thy God; It is he that giveth thee power

## The Midas Touch

The wealth-multiplying benefits of Calvinist Christianity were realized only in northern Europe, England, and America. All other nations have enjoyed crumbs from the Calvinist table. Non-Christian nations, such as Japan, are enjoying prosperity today, but only to the extent that they modify their economies to agree with the covenant of Christ. Communistic and socialist anti-Christian economies are collapsing, because they are in competition with the products of Calvinistic capitalism. This is not a revolutionary or unknown doctrine. Max Weber wrote of this years ago, but anti-Christian bias has thwarted many obvious applications. Even the term, "Protestant work ethic," sticks in the throats of many anti-Christian intellectuals. When they are compelled to mention the Calvinist Protestant work ethic, they substitute "work ethic," so as not to offend the Social Marxism lurking in the hearts of an unproductive academia. The word of God is very clear when the law of God is applied in every area of our lives, "... whatsoever he doeth shall prosper" (Psalm 1:3). Here is the Midas touch!

Marxism or anti-Christian humanism, on the other hand, refuses to recognize the demonstrated wealth-creating power of obeying the Ten Commandments. I was taught as a student that people got wealthy by robbing, exploiting, and taking advantage of the underclass. In all my academic experience, even in Christian schools and a Christian college, only one professor under whom I studied was pro-capitalist with a pro-Christian bias. That was Dr. Stuart Crane of Bob Jones University. The best that could be said about the rest of my teachers was that they were ignorant about the wealth-producing blessings of Calvinism. Perhaps they were silent for fear of religious persecution. For make no mistake about it, the professor who dares to speak in favor of Calvinism will be ruthlessly persecuted unless he owns the school.

## The Evil of Silence

To know these realities and to remain silent is both a great sin and a terrible evil. Our young should be taught that wealth multiplies with obedience to God's law. Some of my teachers were not conscious evil doers but merely ignorant, because teachers do not usually experience the business world. They are either governmental employees or secular religious employees of various anti-Christian faiths. Therefore, they teach their students that the highest service to God is service to mankind, either in the government or some nonprofit organization. I have learned to define anti-Calvinist as any organization not wholeheartedly in favor of applying God's law-word to every area of life. Unfortunately, a pervasive but often unconscious hatred of Calvinism permeates every level of American society.

For example, recently one of my teachers was falsely accused of paddling students. The local television stations and the newspaper immediately jumped in the battle against Grace Community Schools. A newspaper reporter phoned me long distance almost daily demanding information about any tax privileges granted to our organization. I pointed out to the angry reporter that a local property tax exemption is granted to all school organizations, both church and non-church, and that furthermore, a property tax exemption in our case only equaled the annual gross income from one student. He then proceeded with a long list of questions, centering on the growth of Grace Community Schools, how much property we owned, and so on. I then asked, "Mr. X, if I am able to provide child care and in addition, all of the wonderful educational benefits that we offer at no additional charge, where are the victims you are trying to protect?"

There was no reply, so I said, "The answer, my friend, is that no one is being ripped off, because my tuition is as low or lower than my competitors, and my parents have enrolled their children freely at my schools. My teachers earn more than teachers in comparable institutions. Please tell me who is being ripped off here?"

The reporter replied, "I see what you mean." He then asked other questions. When his newspaper articles appeared, there was no reference to my question, nor my answer, because they would have revealed that I was a benefactor and not the villain that he wanted to portray.

## Religious Persecution

The fires of such persecution may sometime sear all Godly entrepreneurs, but as Meshach, Shadrach, and Abednego (Daniel 3:12-30) were joined in the fire by the Son of God, so will all those who choose the way of God's law instead of the way of the world. Although you may not enjoy the good opinion of the anticapitalist bigots in society and the church, you will enjoy great wealth in this life and in the life to come. The God of the Bible wishes "above all things that thou mayest prosper and be in health, even as thy soul prospereth" (III John 2). Decide to provide a true education using our system. The bad opinion of the Pharisees is a small, small price to pay.

## Providing a True Education

What is a true education? To a modern teacher who follows his humanistic training, it is primarily social adjustment. Academic skills are important, but not as important as learning to "fit in," not to be a bigot, always to believe and follow the majority and such "important" skills.

First, to an orthodox Christian, the goal is to read the Bible independently. Why? Well, the orthodox Christian believes that only Christ can save. Since the child cannot save himself, he must be led to the Bible, for it is his only hope. After the child has been taught basic facts, such as the resurrection, the Commandments, the Lord's Prayer, and the Twenty-third Psalm, then literacy becomes a "holy obligation," not an option to the Christian teacher. For this reason, universal education had its origin with the Protestant Reformation and Martin Luther in particular. Without literacy, the child can be robbed of maximum opportunity for a full reward. Christians debate free will in salvation, but all Christians (or nearly all) agree that man can choose after his new birth to submit or not submit to Christ. Romans 12:1: "I beseech you therefore, brethren, by the mercies of God, that ye present your bodies a living sacrifice, holy, acceptable unto God, which is your reasonable service."

### Success Can Be Easily Won by Our Children

The second goal to an orthodox Christian is adjustment to the commandments of God, not to the majority. If the majority of people in the child's life are cannibals, whoremongers, drunks, drug addicts, or thieves, we certainly would not want the child to socially adjust, would we? (especially if adjustment means being a well-adjusted criminal). Given the moral blank taught in government schools or antinomian Christian schools, this is about what can be expected. A true education is very dependent on the parent's choice of school. We Christians should not despair about our amoral society, because the systemic ignorance of our culture represents great opportunity for our children, provided they are truly educated. If they can be honest among thieves, chaste among fornicators, drug and alcohol free among those enslaved to substances, literate among those who cannot read above the fifth-grade level, etc., our children can more easily win success. "In the land of the blind, the one-eyed man is king." The genuine and literate Christian can easily best all rivals.

## More Than Conquerors

True education must be an education that equips the child to compete in a very competitive world. Humanists, socialists, and various shades of collectivist mentality dream of a world of endless cooperation in which everyone works for the common good, sharing freely the labor of their hands with all people equally. The recent collapse of the Soviet Union is only the most recent tower of such nonsense to collapse. Private property is supported by the Word of God. Two of the Ten Commandments—"Thou shalt not steal," and "Thou shalt not covet"— directly support private property. For this reason, all socialist schemes run counter to reality, and we must educate our children to be sane. It is insanity to try to build a world that is imaginary with imaginary common ownership of property. It cannot be done. Private ownership, on the other hand, rewards the productive and creative worker more than the failure. Failures scream in anger at God and attempt to pull down the world of private property. As the old Jewish proverb goes, "He that does not give his child a trade trains him to be a thief." Socialists are thieves using government bureaucracy backed up by storm troopers, instead of knives, clubs, and guns in a dark alley.

## Education for the Real World

The artificial world created by the anti-Christian, pro-socialist mentality that has created our school system has desperately tried to eliminate competition. When I was in grade school in the Pittsburgh school system in the 1940s, various subjects were graded satisfactory and unsatisfactory. When I transferred to a rural district outside of Pittsburgh in the fifth grade, the local school system graded by numbers, 85 and above for a B, 92 and above for an A. By the time my children entered the same rural system twenty-five years later, grading by numbers was obsolete, and credit was being given in mathematics for wrong answers if the methodology was correct.

By the time I was principal of a private, Christian school, I hired three graduates in a single year from Princeton University. When I looked at the transcripts of their college work, I was surprised to note that all of them had graduated with honors. Then turning over the transcript, I found the explanation. The majority of the students graduating from Princeton graduated with honors. It seems the major competition is getting into an exclusive school. Once inside, grade inflation has watered-down everything except perhaps the hard sciences and mathematics. I say, perhaps, because the math teacher I hired from Princeton was not superior to the caliber of math teachers I had hired from less esteemed universities. When I attended graduate schools, the average grade was a B. Any grade less than B was considered failing. So typically, every student in my graduate classes obtained a B or an A without any competition. The goal of the modern educator is to reduce competition in every way possible and to make all students as equal as possible. All must be equal: black, yellow, red and white, stupid, gifted and perverted; all must be equal in the eyes of a false collectivist god.

Everybody a winner; nobody a loser. There is one area, however, where the liberal, anti-Christian leveling process has not been so successful and that is sports.

## Sports: A Game Closer to Real Life

It is nearly impossible to tell an underdeveloped, butterfingered, uncoordinated child that he is a winner, because feedback on the athletic field is immediate. No amount of positive thinking, self-esteem psychobabble can overcome immediate feedback. The difference between winning and losing on the athletic field is very close to the game of life in the real world outside academic circles. For this reason, at Grace Community Schools we insert competition into every possible moment of the child's day. Math games, word games, spelling bees, recognition for the best behaved, most original, most creative, etc. We even have a contest to see who the leader will be to lead us out to bathroom break, or snack time, because competition is the element that the Lord has inserted into His world. No castles in the air can change reality. Our competition extends also onto the playground with hopscotch, foot races, jumping contests, ring-a-round the rosy, and organized activities; not the disorganized chaos that is found on the public school playground. Games have rules that must be obeyed, especially when prizes are to be won, and recognition lost by those who cannot discipline themselves to follow the rules to win the prize. This is God's world, and there are special curses on the heads of all educators who encourage children to become (good) losers in God's world. In our manual are more detailed explanations of how to be winners in God's world.

## Add Structure to Add Security

Incidentally, children are far happier in a world of order than a world of chaos. Rules known and administered justly produce security for the child. Children are born into a world that is terribly frightening, because they do not know what is going to happen. The future could bring disaster, sorrow, and failure, and in too many of their homes, the future has already brought arguments, divorce, and drunkenness. Often their meals are not served on a regular, predictable schedule. Some children come from homes that are an existential hell on earth. At Grace Community, on the other hand, every moment of every day is scheduled. The rules are the same every day. Every day the teachers are predictable. The child can depend on this world, and he can depend on how to proceed into the future in the world of Grace Community and emerge triumphant. Structure, in other words, brings security to the child.

Remove the structure and we create an insecure child. I use the word "structure" for order, scheduling, and predictable events, because this is precisely what many of my educational instructors despised. They hate structure. They argue that structure stifles creativity. The opposite is the case. In an unpredictable world, where the child doesn't know what is happening next, in a world where the child doesn't know what will be workable ten minutes from now, how can he create a better way? He has no base line of an existing world. Add structure and you add security to the child and counter the unstructured, insecure home life that threatens his development.

## Immediate Feedback of Music

Music instruction is a key part of the Grace Community curriculum, because the wrong note, like the poorly thrown pass or badly bunted ball, yields immediate feedback. It is not an accident that modern music becomes more and more atonal and chaotic, because the nihilistic liberal wants to remove all rules. For example, in one school I administered we developed a championship high school band program. Incidentally, this was easy to do. We simply added an extra period to the school day and made the extra period mandatory band practice on a daily basis. The reason that most children do not master a musical instrument is because they are not disciplined to practice long enough to sharpen their skills to the point where music becomes pleasurable. What a structured system does is substitute the teacher's discipline and longer attention span for the student's undiscipline and shorter span.

## Lend the Child Your Discipline

If the teacher is patient, systematic, and persistent, the students' discipline and concentration will lengthen; and positive feedback will result.

To return to my narrative, when we took our championship band to compete against the public schools in the state of Maryland, our disciplined youngsters easily bested all rivals. When our students cheered when their first-place rating was announced, the public school music officials were very offended. They pulled aside our teachers and scolded them, saying, "Don't you people realize that this is a music festival, not a competition?" So, the assault on Christ's orderly world is even fought in the world of music.

Of course, similar things have happened in the world of poetry. Rhythm and rhyme have been all but banished from modern poems and what can we say about modern art? The attack on reality here is too obvious to merit comment. The Christian preschool is an opportunity to bring as much health-giving stability as possible into the lives of the little children in the event they enter into the existential nightmare called "public education."

## A Perfect World to See and Hear

Systematic phonics and music instruction teach the child that a beautiful and predictable world exists where discipline is rewarded, and sloth is punished. The child will be able to hear language, not just see it. He will be able to sense and feel the rhythm of language, all of which teaches the predestinated kingdom of God. Without such instruction, it is difficult for the child to see the kingdom of God and reach out for faith to believe and search for that perfect world that is coming with the victory of all those who have eyes to see and ears that hear.

These are only a few of the secrets of success found in our system. Apply the operational manual as directed, and good things will happen. But what about government interference? Won't there be opposition?

# CHAPTER VIII
# What About Government Regulations?

It is the responsibility of the potential school owner to get a copy of the specific regulations that apply in his state. In several states, as in Florida, the Christian schools have pressured their state legislatures into certain concessions. Be on guard concerning the reluctance of your state bureaucrats to volunteer the existence of exceptions in your state.

When I started in Florida, I was told point-blank lies by the state employee about the exceptions for Christian schools. As providence kindly ordained, however, I signed up for the state-mandated training course early. Usually, the candidate to operate a daycare takes the course after it is in operation. During the course, the state supervisor warned us to have our state permit number printed on all of our advertising. One of the students asked why a private school in our town did not display their number. She replied, "Oh, they belong to a private association that is given recognition in Tallahassee [Florida's state capital]." I was startled, to say the least. This same state supervisor had told me twice that there were no exceptions! The following day, after a few long-distance phone calls, I discovered that I had been deceived. Thus, do not take every government official's word at face value. Phone other schools and discover from your future colleagues the true governmental climate.

I seldom talk about starting a Christian school by using a daycare as a base that someone doesn't challenge me from the floor or after the presentation with skeptical questions, prefaced by, "Don't you know that the government...?" Apparently, I fail to convince some listeners that I am aware of government sins or that I fail to warn sufficiently about governmental potential for harassment. I am well aware from both study and painful personal experience of government prejudice and opposition to any Christian work. I have been jailed twice for open-air preaching. I have been unsuccessfully recommended for prosecution in the state of Maryland. Despite these experiences, I have learned that the government cannot prevent our entrance into the marketplace, nor can they drive us away, provided we are brave enough to try intelligently. Handwringing about governmental abuse, although very real, does a disservice to the Christian school movement. We play into the hands of our enemy if we paint our enemy as so strong that it seems useless to resist. When I talk with people in non-Christian daycare, I am amused at the similarity of their complaints to ours. Bureaucrats are petty and vicious to everyone, Christian and non-Christian alike. We must be wiser and more rational than those without faith. In fact, there is a very positive benefit to governmental persecution that you may not have considered.

The bureaucrat bars entry and drives weak competitors from the market. If you are strong, they are helping you! Don't despair! Let the faint of heart be driven off; that just makes room for more serious Christians to have more students to teach. The so-called "survival of the fittest" assists Christians. We have found that bureaucrats are well aware of public opinion. Offset their suspicion by being friendly and cooperative. Offer some refreshments. Ask about their families, their church, their hobbies, etc. Most people are disarmed by such questions. Nothing demonstrates friendliness better than listening with interest to the answers to such questions. Ask for advice. Say, "I am sorry, I wasn't aware of that regulation. If you were me, how would you solve this problem?" For example, I was angrily told by a government worker in New Hampshire that I had to take down a school sign advertising our Open House. I replied, "Oh, this is terrible. We have thousands of dollars in direct mail asking people to come here this weekend. What would you do in this situation?"

She looked at me thoughtfully and seeing that I was not antagonistic but genuinely interested, she replied, "Well, Reverend, I would get a sandwich board sign painted and set that up at the intersection. Someone will no doubt complain, but by the time I hear about it, you could already have it down." I thanked her sweetly. We used that sandwich sign with great effectiveness again and again. Be friendly. Satan has trouble with his help just as the church does.

CHAPTER IX
# Advice on Corporate Structure

The strongest protection against government interference (although it is declining) is to have your school under the aegis of a church. This arrangement operates with the church as the corporation and the school as a registered fictitious name with your county. The church arrangement offers the most danger for losing control, however, and also prevents you from passing ownership of your school to your children. But there is a way to enjoy the benefits of both.

Lease your school to the church. In this manner, if the church attempts to interfere in the operation of the school, you can cancel the lease and as quick as lightning, you are free. Your lease arrangement would simply state, "one dollar and other valuable considerations." The property would be in your name. In many states, it is not necessary that the property be in the church's name in order to qualify for property tax exemption. It is enough that the property be used for "religious purposes." Check carefully what the laws in your state are before establishing your school.

Another arrangement is to incorporate your school independently of a church. Under a church's aegis, you don't have to file a form 990 with the IRS, but under this arrangement, you will. This is just an information return, but it is still necessary to go to the expense and bother. The disadvantage with this arrangement is that, just as under a church as a nonprofit corporation, you will have a board that can give you control problems and inheritance cannot be made to your children.

A third arrangement is as a "for profit" corporation. Under this arrangement, control is not a problem, but your tax bite is higher. The taxes are not the problem you may think, however, since both the taxes and depreciation can be used as deductible expenses on your federal tax return.

There are other alternatives, of course—sole proprietorship, partnership, etc. Your final choice will and should be made only with careful advice, depending upon your personal situation. There is one choice I never advise anyone to take and that is to place a church in both ownership and control of your school. It is heartbreaking to talk with ministers who suddenly wake up in their old age to the fact that they cannot provide for their widows and children after their demise. Too late they realize that a lifetime of work and devotion will pass to people who do not know, understand, and appreciate the blood, sweat, and tears that go into building a school. If a minister reads this and decides consciously to disinherit his family hoping to gain the Lord's favor, consider the verse, Prov. 13:22: "A good man leaveth an inheritance to his children's children."

One of my best friends in the ministry foresaw that he was dying and that his family would not benefit from the church and school he started from scratch 20 years before. When I discussed this chapter with him, he said, "I wish I had had this conversation twenty years ago. I would have done things differently!" Unfortunately, his worst fears came true. His family did realize very little from the $3-4 million dollars' worth of property left to the control of men who did not know their pastor very long, did not work with their pastor for long, and, I am afraid, will not remember his family for long. Ministers who are bound by oaths of celibacy can justify such thoughtless foolishness, but men who have families should remember that, "But if any provide not for his own and specially for those of his own house, he hath denied the faith, and is worse than an infidel" (I Tim. 5:8).

A preacher should retain the property for his school in his own name and lease it to a not-for-profit corporation if he wishes to retain tax benefits, such as a housing allowance and exemption from social security. The school structure outlined in my operational manual can achieve enough profit so that donations are not needed as in other schools. Therefore, do not solicit or accept donations. Don't sell magazines, candy, seeds, etc. Finance your school by selling your service, i.e., education. By refusing to beg, you will keep anyone or any group from believing they can dictate to your school. You will also force yourself to operate at a surplus (profit). You will charge the market price for your service. The market will be your measure and guide. When and if the government audits your books, no one can claim you gouged anyone! You accepted money given in exchange for a service. On the other hand, if you take money from donors, you open yourself to the suspicion of private inurement. A school does not have to operate as a begging church. A church should not sell its services, but a school can and should sell its services.

By means of a school, a minister can achieve financial independence and accumulate an estate for his family. I know of no better way that this can be done than mine. Building a school is a unique opportunity.

## CHAPTER X
# My Personal Testimony

From the previous chapters, I hope that you, as a present or future educator, are persuaded to establish your own school to achieve financial independence and security for yourself and your family. I hope you see that this is a good and proper motive. But the only motive that can be blessed of the Lord is to sincerely seek first to extend the dominion of Christ. Matt. 6:33 is crystal clear that only the one who seeks first the profit of Christ can expect profit for himself; that is, wealth gotten in the way of righteousness. Solomon, for example, prayed first for wisdom to do his calling as king of Israel, and the Lord subsequently added unto him great wealth. Likewise, we must pray first to have the Lord's wisdom to teach correctly our students, so we may have a legitimate hope of material wealth. We are called as Christian teachers to extend the territory of Christ's dominion into the hearts of those young who have been given to Christ by God the Father.

The gospel, however, has been greatly polluted and confused in our age. Our gospel has been watered-down by permissiveness masquerading as love, which has all but vanquished the Biblical fear of God necessary for the beginning of wisdom (see Prov. 1:9). It is a very old heresy: "Love conquers all." Combined with this distortion of the Gospel is the falsehood that the sinner has power to affect his own salvation by our Lord Jesus Christ.

This may be confusing to some, so let me illustrate my meaning from personal experience.

### How the Lord Taught the Gospel to Me

I was reared in the Presbyterian church, but it was a church that was lukewarm concerning the authority of the Bible. I recall attending a Billy Graham revival at Forbes Field in Pittsburgh as a teenager of 15. A busload of adults and teens from our church was transported to the stadium from Rennerdale, a suburb of Pittsburgh. I understood as I listened to the very eloquent Reverend Graham that my sins could be washed away if I responded to the "invitation" at the end of the sermon. Curious, I wanted to "go forward," but none of the others in our group was responding; and I was concerned whether I would ever be able to find our bus afterward in the largest, most confusing crowd I had ever seen in my young life. Therefore, I contented myself with quietly praying the "Sinner's Prayer." In a very contemplative mood, I boarded the bus for the trip home. Near me, I could hear the Sunday School superintendent and the pastor in earnest conversation. The pastor asked if anyone had gone forward. The superintendent replied, "No, I checked the seats and the passenger list carefully. We can go."

"Good," cried the pastor, with an excited and pleased tone to his voice. "Everyone who joins the Presbyterian church has to confess that they believe the death, burial, and resurrection of Christ and that the Bible is the Word of God. There is no need for any of us to respond to such an invitation."

I settled back in my seat and thanked what I thought were my lucky stars that I had not made a fool of myself. I continued on with all of the normal weaknesses endemic to the youth of my age. During the coming years, however, I was bothered by the pastor's certainty that none of us needed to respond to such an invitation.

## My First Religious Experience

I thought back to the earliest memory that could be termed a religious experience. I was four years old, seated in a pew of a Free Methodist church, beside my younger brother and my mother. My mother had taken us to church, not of our own free choice. She had been ordered to take us to church by my father, who as far as I could remember throughout my youth and young adulthood, never personally attended church or anything of a religious nature, except for weddings and funerals. Surprisingly, this lukewarm Presbyterian ordered his Italian Roman Catholic wife to take those boys to church. "All children need to go to church," I remember him saying. By church, he didn't mean Roman Catholic, so my mother packed us up on Sunday morning, and we walked two blocks east on Steuben Street in Pittsburgh to the first Protestant church available. As predestinated, I am sure, the church was very conservative, a Free Methodist congregation. In 1939, the Free Methodists had no instrumental music. I can remember before the congregation sang very sad hymns, a leader would step forward and strike a note on a pitch pipe. That was the last clear and beautiful note to be heard. In my young mind, that was hilarious. The only other thing I remember about the Free Methodist congregation besides the fact that they were quite old and that no young children attended the pastor's sermon, was the pastor's usual benediction. He would raise both hands high in the air with the palms facing the congregation, repeat Numbers 6:24-26, "The Lord bless thee and keep thee. The Lord make His face shine upon thee and be gracious unto thee. The Lord lift up His countenance upon thee and give thee peace. Amen."

The idea of sunshine from the face of the Lord fascinated me. I peppered my mother with questions. She told me that the pastor had power to bless his flock, that from his hands to us passed a blessing by God. The following week, I sneaked a peek to see if I could see the blessing. Of course, I couldn't, but the notion remained in my mind.

### Off to Church, Pajamas and All

My next religious experience came three years later, when I was seven. We had moved about two miles across the suburb of Elliott to a new home. The habit of going to church stopped with the move. I woke up on a Sunday morning uneasy about not going to church. I bounded across the hall to where my mother and father lay getting some Sunday morning extra sleep time. My mother mumbled, "Go back to bed."

I replied, "Can we go to church after you get up?" Irritated, my father growled, "Go back to bed." Dejected, I moped back down the hall to the second story front bedroom that I shared with my younger brother. It was a beautiful sunny morning. I looked out the bedroom window. The canvas awning had been put up, and I decided it would be great fun to crawl out of the window, slide down the awning, and drop to the patch of grass and shrubbery below. When I hit the ground, I recall spots in front of my eyes and trouble regaining my breath, but when my wind returned, I was unhurt, outside and free to go to church. The only problem was that I was still in my pajamas, but that didn't seem a handicap to my young mind.

I started down the hill to find my Free Methodist church. I knew how to get there, because my mother had made the same walk with us several times. When I got to the bottom of the hill, about five blocks from my home, I passed a church by the name of Evangelical Free Church. From the open windows, I could hear piano music and singing. The music was much better than the Free Methodist, and it was still a long, long walk uphill to get to the very sad hymns with sadder disharmony of the Methodists, so I turned into the Evangelical church. I was met at the door by a male deacon who assumed that I was a youngster who lived down the alley from the church. Apparently, he and another deacon had called door-to-door in the neighborhood, trying to get new children for Sunday School.

He was delighted that I came in my pajamas. He thought it was wonderful and ushered me immediately into a class of children my age. I was astonished. The church basement was filled with children all singing and "carrying on." During the Sunday School lesson, the teacher went over their Gospel, using John 3:16. I listened with intense interest and excitedly started asking questions. She seemed delighted until she heard the questions. I asked, "Just this past week, my brother and I saw a dead man in a house two doors from us lying in a casket with people crying. Do you mean to tell me that if that poor man believed in Jesus, he would not have died?"

The woman began to stammer and tried to clarify what she meant by "never die." Unsatisfied, I continued to challenge her concept of death. Finally, an ugly little boy began to make fun of me, by saying how stupid I was. "Everyone knows what she is talking about except you. You stupid little Dago! Where do you live anyway?" It was true I looked like my beautiful Italian mother rather than my Scotch-Irish father, but "Dago" was a fighting word for me.

With one hand, I reached across the table, wound my hand in his loose shirt, and with the other, I started to punch.

With satisfaction, I noticed that his nose began to bleed. The screaming teacher managed to summon the door-to-door evangelist/deacon to pull me off the ugly antagonist. Now banished from the classroom, I was made to sit in the back of the assembly hall with the deacon as my guard. He asked me what had happened, and I told him as best I could. He urged me to stay to see the pastor between Sunday School and church. I tried to leave, but the deacon grabbed me and pushed me back into the chair; so finally, I submitted to the long wait.

When the Sunday School was over, the deacon ushered me into the pastor's office. The pastor listened to what the deacon had to say and then asked me for an explanation. I replied that I was just curious as to the difference between death and whatever the Sunday School teacher thought was death and life. Also, I said I had been interrupted in my questions by another little boy who called me a "Dago." The pastor turned furious. It seemed the ugly little boy was his son. The pastor didn't believe I had any interest at all in salvation. He intended to take me home by the scuff of my neck right after church so that my parents could properly punish me. The deacon took me to the back of the church, and the worship service began. As he stood for the beginning of the service, I darted for the door. To my relief, this time, he didn't pursue me or try to grab me. And home I went.

Walking up the hill, I thought within myself, "Well, it must be true that some people who believe in Jesus must never die, but those would only be those who would be sons of God. Too bad," thought I, "that I am not a son of God." Suddenly, I had an urge to look upward in the sky. From inside my mind, I heard a very quiet voice say, "Ellsworth, you are my son." But just as quickly, I thought it was my imagination. I dismissed the vision, for I had always been a very imaginative youth, prone when younger to confuse my vivid imagination with real life events. So, I chalked it up to imagination.

When I returned home, my mother was disgraced that I had gone to church in my pajamas, but this time, to my surprise, I was not even paddled, just sternly warned that more unauthorized church attendance would result in a beating and a near-death experience. I promised very loudly and sincerely to not "run away," as she put it, again.

## Born Again at Thirty

My next religious experience took place the week between Christmas and New Year's, 1964. My anticommunist activities had led me to several appearances on television. I was a 30-year-old life insurance general agent, and together with a 26-year-old radio announcer executive, we had formed a pressure group to expose several civil rights leaders of the '60s as communist-inspired. As each civil rights leader came to town, we would research and print up their communist-front citations, hold a press conference, and distribute the information to the media. So far, we had been successful enough to prevent Pittsburgh from the riotous burnings that occurred in more than 64 other cities at the time. To our surprise, however, B'nai B'rith announced in the paper that they, together with the Anti- Defamation League, would expose my friend and me, as well as a Rev. Dr. W. O. H. Garman, as bigots. They charged us with being Jew-hating bigots who wrapped ourselves in the flag and waved the Bible. Astonished, we could not understand how opposing black people with communist connections equaled hating Jewish people of whom we had never heard. We entered quietly into the back of the meeting hall in the Hotel Webster in the Oakland section of Pittsburgh to hear ourselves characterized as hatemongering extremists. The extremist label was somewhat new to us. Just as soon as I seated myself, a plump Jewish woman who looked like Molly Goldberg from a television sitcom, turned and dilated her large, brown eyes, snapped her head backwards, and in a stage whisper, said to the woman next to her, "Don't look now. There is a big extremist sitting behind us."

We didn't take her seriously. It seemed at first bizarre and humorous, but before the evening was over, we realized that the speakers were not humorous but in dead earnest in their hatred for us. It is important to report to the reader that the speakers attacking us were not all Jews. Several were liberal clergy from large Christian churches. It is a profound mistake to think that the enemies of Christianity are all from one race or faith. Just as the children of God are of ". . . every kindred, and tongue and people and nation;" (Rev. 5:9), so are His enemies.

The following Tuesday, I received a phone call from the coordinator of the John Birch Society, telling me that the Rev. Garman would be answering the B'nai B'rith in his Wednesday evening prayer service. I attended the service, which turned out to be a communion service as well. The pastor, ever smiling, calmly related that the Jews were God's chosen people, that we had to lovingly understand and bring them to Christ, and that in their spiritual blindness, they were opposing themselves and confusing their friends with their enemies as we had before our conversion to Christ. After some more of this line of thought buttressed with many lines of Scripture references, I was impressed with how intelligently the pastor used the Bible to support his points. I had risen to be Sunday School superintendent of my Presbyterian church; and throughout my regular attendance at the church, the Bible was ponderously quoted, maybe a verse or two of unintelligible words, at the beginning of a 20–30-minute discourse of standard humanism, brotherhood, equality, and such, with no further notice or need to refer back to the Bible at all. The idea that the Bible could be used as a source of ideas or proofs to buttress current thinking impressed me.

Now as the communion service began, the pastor sternly warned that only a genuine believer in Christ dared to partake in the body and blood symbolically represented. I partook, saying to myself, "I have served as a Sunday School superintendent, I have been a Presbyterian all my adult life, so surely I believe as well as can be expected."

Now came time to partake of the grape juice. The pastor repeated his warning. I lifted the tiny cup to my lips, trembled a little, and returned it untouched to the rack on the back of the pew. On the way out of the church, I shook hands with the genial, smiling pastor and returned home.

A few weeks before this incident, my wife had reported to me that she had been warned of the Lord in a quiet voice that the children needed to attend church. I had recently been forced out of the Presbyterian church of my youth, because the new pastor and some of the members of the congregation had wanted to excommunicate me for distributing literature to the members of the church, saying that the Rev. Martin Luther King had pro-communist affiliations and friends. My wife's vision and voice of God or not, I was determined not to send my children to a church that wanted to excommunicate their father for only being what was in his mind a patriot. So, I phoned Rev. Garman and asked him if he had a Sunday School since the church was very tiny. Also, I asked if he taught the Bible from the anticommunist viewpoint that I heard in his Wednesday service. Yes, he had a Sunday School, he replied, but no, he couldn't teach the Bible from the perspective that I wanted unless he had a special class of at least 10 people. I assured him that I could get a class of 10 people together and that I would be at his church on Wednesday evenings to hear him teach.

    I gathered my wife, my radio announcer friend and his wife, my mother and father, an insurance salesman who worked for me, and Alice, the wife of the coordinator of the John Birch Society. It was not quite the 10, but it was close enough to astonish the smiling pastor. I didn't realize it at the time, but the ability to get up such a group to attend a Bible study was a nearly impossible sales feat. He was delighted to start the class. For his textbook, he chose a pamphlet entitled, "Dispensational Truths" by C. I. Scofield, and week by week, we covered the "dispensations" with very interesting lectures, linking Bible applications to contemporary events occurring in America and the world. Most of us were convinced that the Christian cause was lost, and that communism would eventually triumph. There was no comfort in the smiling pastor's grim assessment. He assured us that we should rejoice that things were getting worse and worse. This only meant that the Lord was returning soon to rescue us from the Great Tribulation, which doubtlessly lay just ahead. Interestingly, as I look back now, none of us took him seriously enough to quit the anticommunist movement, fold our hands over our laps, and wait for the Lord's return. Instead, we were determined to be martyrs to our patriotic dreams now made even more shining and wonderful by the Christian trappings found in the pastor's words.

    About the week of the fifth lesson, the telephone rang in my insurance office on the tenth floor of the Manor Building in downtown Pittsburgh. On the other end of the phone was Alice, the Birch official's wife. She, in her excited Boston Irish accent, related how this lesson seemed to teach all one had to do was to call upon the Lord and one could be assured of everlasting life.

Alice apparently had many alcoholic Irish friends who attended AA meetings. She observed that only those who claimed to be "born again" seemed to get sober and stay sober, but she doubted the whole thing. What did I think? I replied that I had just finished reading the lesson, and there had to be 30 Bible verses quoted, all supporting the notion that salvation was by faith alone and that if I were you, I would take the Lord at His word. She gasped in astonishment, "Then you believe this?"

I said, "Of course, how can I doubt it?" The conversation ended. As I returned the phone to its rack, I thought within myself, "How very cool and confident I was when talking to her. Just as a former Sunday School superintendent should be, I suppose, but how could I be so very sure? How could I know that what the Bible said was reliable?" I rose and turned to the large window in my office, overlooking the city and the Monongahela River and Mt. Washington beyond. I said to myself, "It has to be true, because God doesn't lie." In that second, I saw from the sky columns of light descending here and there all over the city. None over the water of the river nor on the rugged mountainside, but some up high on top of Mt. Washington. I perceived that the columns of light were descending upon people. It was not an indiscriminate sunshine. In front of me, I now perceived someone just on the other side of the window, looking through the glass at me. I couldn't make out the features. Something was smeared on the glass. I heard a voice say, "Come out from behind there."

In an instant, I departed from my body. Astonished, I looked back at my body, and then experienced wonderful, radiant heat much like sunshine, but a light that seemed to have marvelous healing and soothing characteristics. I was naked, but not ashamed and hilariously I began to dance, twirling around and round like a child in wild joy. Suddenly, bundles of sticks were falling about my dancing feet. Greedily, I gathered the bundles as fast as I could. I had all but one of them. Looking back dejectedly on the missing bundle, I reluctantly had to return to my body. Somewhat like a rubber band snaps back into its place, I was back, and the vision was over. This experience at 30 years of age was not as easily dismissed as my previous experiences. I was totally persuaded that this was real. Since the pastor had pumped us full of expectations that Jesus was returning at any moment, I resolved that this must be the Lord's return. I bounded out of my office into the bullpen area where my agents were seated. At the top of my voice, I said, "Why are you sitting there? Didn't you see that?"

Puzzled, they said, "See what?"

For the first time, I realized that my vision was a private matter. Embarrassed, I mumbled, "Never mind," and retreated to my office.

## Why Was All This Experience Not Enough?

Let's review what should be a soul-satisfying list of religious experiences and a crackerjack vision of a magnitude to make a charismatic's heart go pitter-patter—from my earliest fascination with the power of a pastor's benediction to my pre-puberty zeal to delve the mystery of John 3:16 in my pajamas, my teenage experience at a Billy Graham revival, and now an authentic vision of heavenly sunshine at the age of 30, certainly these events would be the clearest and strongest proof of being born again? Or were they? Almost as quickly as I was able to dismiss the voice and vision from the clouds proclaiming to a seven-year-old in pajamas that he was indeed a son of God, doubts quickly arose within me about the genuineness of my salvation.

Dr. Garman's church had a tract rack. I remember scooping up about a dozen tracts and sitting down to compare them with each other and with my experience. None seemed to me to correlate with my vision of heavenly sunshine. As a matter of fact, some of the tracts sternly warned against basing hope of eternal life on emotions. Uncomfortably, I felt that my experiences had given me an emotional "rush," but didn't seem the quality that carried the historical martyrs to the stake. No matter how often I reviewed my experiences or reprayed the "Sinner's Prayer" or told myself that I did indeed believe in the death, burial, and resurrection of Christ, doubts remained. I read more gospel tracts by Oliver Greene, John R. Rice, and Theodore Epp, the Back to the Bible Broadcaster, so that I knew the four simple steps of salvation and the gospel (so-called) very well indeed. "When all else fails, read the instructions," say the sages.

At last, I set aside the tracts and the commentators and read the Bible. Very much like Mark Twain's famous wisecrack, "What I didn't understand didn't bother me; but oh, what I did understand bothered me a great deal!" I found, for example, salvation was indeed by faith alone, but I Corinthians 15 spoke of different kinds of faith, one vain and another genuine. Which did I have? It was a frightening question.

## Mother Goose Religion

In Rev. Garman's church, a sermon or Sunday School lesson never seemed to pass without numerous direct or indirect assurances that "We are not under law but under grace." Yet I found the Lord Jesus Christ warning "Not one jot or tittle of the law shall pass" and that anyone who taught that the law was done away would be least in His eyes. I also discovered that, contrary to my church's constant emphasis on the love of God, the Bible's emphasis was on the fear of God. I noted that Scofield nimbly ducked this one by a footnote, defining "fear" as "reverential awe," but it was obvious that the Scripture was teaching more than just respectful fear. I noted, for example, that we called a pastor "reverend," but he was lucky to get the respect accorded to the IRS. In practice, the pastor was regarded as a Mother Goose figure or more accurately, a Mother Goose representative, God being the Mother Goose with neither the representative nor the goose to be feared. Instead, both goose and goose representative waited helplessly for us to return their love.

I suspected that my secret, nagging doubts were shared by other church members, because every evangelist and guest speaker seemed to have a common goal, which was to reassure us again and again that Romans 10:13, "For whosoever shall call upon the name of the Lord shall be saved," was all that was required to open heaven's portals when we died.

### The Sermon of a Cold, Stiff Body

About this time, one of our church members died, and the pastor announced the funeral service. I decided to attend. Pastor Garman was an ex-Presbyterian pastor, trained in a Presbyterian seminary, but his undergraduate training was at Philadelphia College of the Bible, an institution founded on the dispensational teaching of the Scofield Bible. Dr. Garman was driven out of the Presbyterian church, because of his fidelity to dispensationalism. I was curious to see how he handled a funeral as compared to the many mainstream Presbyterian funerals of my experience. The one remarkable thing I recall was that Dr. Garman had completely memorized his funeral oration, including great chunks of Scripture, but the thrust of Dr. Garman's memorized oration was to impress his audience with his memorized Bible knowledge and of course, to assure the audience over and over again that the soul of the now dead church member resided safely in the bosom of Christ because of the "Sinner's Prayer." All seemed gratified to be reassured again (this time over a cold, stiff body) that they knew everything necessary to know to escape the burning hell below.

## The Testimony of Converted Drunks

I still wondered and wished that I could believe like my fellow church members seemed to believe. I next began to interview some of them about their salvation hopes. I found the members without serious backgrounds of waywardness had learned a canned testimony similar to the tracts in the rack by the front door, and all my sharp questioning couldn't get them to budge from what they knew was the correct "gospel." The converted Scotch-Irish drunks, on the other hand, always had experiential testimonies very much like my own, except the experiences were individualized. For example, one of the ex-drunks told me that he had been driven in desperation, after many attempts at the "Sinner's Prayer" and trips down the aisle in one city mission after another, to finally collapse on his knees at 3 a.m. beside his flophouse cot and raising one hand toward heaven called upon the Lord. He said a blue, soft light came down from above to his outstretched hand and enveloped his entire body, giving him a peace that had been denied to him before. From that moment, he had been able to stop drinking and that was how he knew that God was his God and heaven was his home, instead of the drunkard's hell he richly deserved.

I interviewed another converted drunk and felon from North Carolina. He related to me that in his hillbilly church, no salvation was worth anything that didn't cause one to "get in the spirit and run for Jesus." He said that, after a life of petty crime and drunkenness, he was seated in the front of a gospel revival service. The Spirit seized him, and he jumped with both feet up on the back of the pew, teetering momentarily on its narrow rim. He then ran across the pews from front to back at breakneck speed with each foot without error landing on the next pew back to the rear of the church, where he bounded out the door and ran screaming for joy, hurling his voice to the heavens until he fell exhausted into the ditch beside the road. There his laughing friends fished him out, brushed him off, and took him home, all rejoicing, because this was absolutely, positively, the authenticated way that real Christians were saved. From that day, he testified he had a new strength to resist sin, which he never had previously. Although he did not become perfect and was not perfect now, he was certain of the power when he repented and sought the Lord to overcome any defect of character, including the one most dreaded in his case, drunkenness. I can still remember his wonderful Southern accent saying, "I got the evidence."

### "Though I Give my Body to be Burned"

I pondered this all in my heart and began to attend revival services at other churches, always seeking that key which seemed to be missing. In a small Baptist church in Midway, Pennsylvania, I heard a "rededication" sermon. I was busy trying to convert my mother and father to my new hope, so I attended the service with my mother, where I heard a message primarily directed toward the group of young people in the front of the congregation headed by their youth pastor. The evangelist said that those young people who had called upon the Lord and were Bible-believing Christians would most likely in their lifetime have the opportunity to become martyrs for Christ. He outlined the advances of the communist menace around the world and particularly in America. It was apparent to me that he was using Birch Society facts and figures and the book None Dare Call It Treason as his source. He was careful not to reveal this to his audience, because the media was pounding constantly on the theme that the John Birchers were the real enemy; and the communists were people we just had to love and understand better, and all our fears would go away.

Well, the evangelist worked his magic and brought the sermon to a thundering conclusion by saying that it was an easy thing to pray the Sinner's Prayer and walk down the aisle in a Baptist church, to call upon the Lord as a fire escape from hell. But the real Christian would be separated from the phony Christian when the jackbooted soldiers would stand in front of a church like this and say, "All those who really believe in Christ remain standing; the rest of you on your faces," while the true believers were mown down in a raining shower of bullets and blood. He said, "Now I am going to give you an invitation that is not so easy to respond to. If you can truthfully say that you are willing to stand to your feet and die for Christ, please stand."

Instantly, I jumped to my feet. The evangelist looked surprised to see a balding 30-year-old on his feet toward the rear of the church, while the young people in front nervously looked around and remained rooted to their seats. He gave the invitation again and this time some others joined. We were all bid to go forward in the church, where the usual simple plan of salvation was tonelessly read by one of the deacons for our affirmation, and we were then dismissed.

On the way home, I thought surely now that I was God's child, security would be mine, since I had committed myself to far more than just the "Sinner's Prayer." I was sincerely committed to be faithful to death, but soon, very soon, the old doubts returned; and I questioned my sincerity and even my good sense and control over my emotions. In the words of the Apostle Paul, "... though I give my body to be burned, and have not charity, it profiteth me nothing" (I Cor. 13:3).

In the months that followed, I prayed often concerning the Lord's will for my life and always the answer seemed to be the Scripture, "But if any provide not for his own, and specially for those of his own house, he hath denied the faith, and is worse than an infidel" (I Tim. 5:8). My only clear perception for me personally was to rear my children in the nurture and admonition of the Lord. This made a Christian school in my mind not an option, but God's law! My pastor, however, could not recommend any Christian school. They are "compromisers," the stern pastor warned. A visiting evangelist, however, did recommend Bob Jones University and a Christian elementary school. What to do? Pittsburgh had been my home all my life. Still, the Lord's command was to rear my children in the fear of God.

While I hesitated, my wife showed me a take-home leaflet from the local public school. My oldest was in the first grade. The parents were to read the leaflet to their children. The leaflet showed a family gathered in prayer. The father wore the Jewish skullcap and on the table was the Hebrew candelabra. The pamphlet instructed the teacher to teach the children about Hanukkah, a wonderful holiday of the Jewish faith when people love one another and exchange gifts. A footnote on the bottom of the leaflet warned that Christian religious instruction was against the law and was forbidden. Isn't it strange, I thought, at Christmas time, my children were forbidden to learn of Christ, but other religions were welcome in my son's classroom?

My hesitation vanished. I set my jaw and resigned my high-paid, unlimited expense account sales job as a trucking company public relations salesman. I led my family to Greenville, South Carolina, to enroll my children in a Christian school. I obtained a similar position with a local trucking company, but after only two weeks of employment, the supervisor fired me, because he received an alarming report that while waiting to interview customers at the various companies that I was scheduled to call upon, it was my custom to read from a pocket New Testament. This was the Bible Belt, and the people are particularly sensitive to nutty Bible believers, who used their positions to hock their religion instead of their wares. To make matters worse, the following Sunday afternoon, while accompanying a member of my Baptist church on a street preaching engagement in front of the city hospital, we were arrested and thrown into jail for the crime of distributing literature on the street, an archaic law that had been in the books since the 1920s against communist organizers of the local textile industry.

The chaplain in the hospital and the district attorney together decided to rid the hospital's public sidewalks of Bible-thumping nuisance preachers. Unfortunately for the district attorney and the chaplain, my large independent Baptist church organized a rally and Dr. Bob Jones, Jr. of the Bob Jones University radio station, interviewed me on the air. The city backed down, but I remained unemployed and had a family of four children to feed. The manager of the Bob Jones University radio station offered me a sales position at a salary which, characteristic of Christian work, was too little to support my family. But I still had the GI educational benefits. The salary combined with the GI bill was enough to keep my children in Christian school and the tin roof of our trailer over our heads.

## How to Find the Lord's Will

That following scenario has been played out many times in my life. The Lord's will is found at the end of the boot that kicks me into the dust; and when I pick myself up, there is only one door open. So it was that I became an advertising salesman for the radio station and a student at Bob Jones University at the age of 31. Meanwhile, I continued to participate in street evangelism. But I was still haunted about the authenticity of my salvation and of the nearly 4,000 professions of faith that street preachers gathered in just one year. I would ask myself how many of the 4,000 were genuinely regenerate and how many just did anything required to shake a persistent holy salesman so they could resume their Saturday shopping.

In my lifelong habit of reading, I came across the testimony of the author of the great hymn, "Amazing Grace," the Rev. John Newton (1725-1807). Newton said that he agonized for a very long time before he believed that he was in grace. Puzzled, I thought to myself that the gospel that we preached on the street was the same as in every evangelical church in America: one could instantly know that he was in grace simply by repeating after the soul winner in the inquiry room the "Sinner's Prayer." Why was John Newton in agony? I opened my hymnal to the words of "Amazing Grace" that every Baptist knows by heart, at least when he is singing it and being prompted by a congregation. The second verse in particular caught my attention. It read, "'Twas grace that taught my heart to fear and grace my fears relieved." Very strange, I thought. The love of God was preached in my church; God was certainly not presented as Someone to fear. We were prompted, so we were told, to come to God because He loved us and died for us and that the least we could do was to respond from the love in our hearts to His greater demonstrated love for us. Too bad, I thought, that John Newton didn't have the benefit of the evolving gospel of our modern day.

Still pondering this question, I entered the large book store of Bob Jones University. Browsing, I came face to face with the manager of the store and told him that I had a large family at home that I wished to lead in family devotions, but I needed a systematic approach to follow to teach my family the basics. I said that in the Presbyterian church I think we had a catechism, although I don't remember ever seeing it, but today I was a saved, born again Baptist. Did the Baptists have anything like a catechism? The manager rummaged around underneath the counter and came up with a small yellow pamphlet, entitled, "Catechism Questions from the Philadelphia Confession of Faith." He said, "This is the Baptist counterpart to the Westminster Catechism to which you referred. He smiled and said, "You can have it for free. God bless you." I took the catechism home and set it on the coffee table in the living room, where it remained for several days.

### The Ways of the Lord are Past Understanding

One morning I awoke late for class, swept into my arms two large glass jugs that I took daily to a nearby dairy farm to get raw milk. (I was a devoted health nut as well as a religious nut.) I stepped out onto an elevated platform (eight feet above the ground) that during the night had been coated with an inch or more of crystal-clear ice. This Pennsylvania boy didn't know what a South Carolina ice storm was all about. Ice covered the porch and all 12 steps to the driveway below. I slid onto my back, holding the two jugs in my arms, terrified that any moment the jugs would break and send glass shards into every part of my upper body. I bounced down the 12 steps headfirst on my back, still clutching the jugs, slamming into the concrete slab below. I hit with such force that all the air was collapsed out of my lungs. With terrible, gasping pain, I recovered my breath, marveling that the jugs were still intact and thinking to myself, "I could have been killed." My wife shrieked from the top of the steps, "Are you OK?" My growling reply was "Yes," and I added, "Obviously, there is going to be no school today since no one could drive on these streets." Just as soon as I could crawl up the icy steps, family devotions would begin with a special thanksgiving for fools sliding down steps trying to keep glass jugs from being broken. This seemed to me an unmistakable sign from the Lord. Don't laugh, because from these family devotions launched that day, I was at last introduced to the gospel according to the Lord Jesus Christ.

The Lord's gospel is different from the watered-down, skimmed version of our day. I read the words under the topic "Of Assurance of Grace and Salvation," Chapter 28 of the Philadelphia Confession of Faith, "This infallible assurance doth not so belong to the essence of faith, but that a true believer may wait long, and conflict with many difficulties before he be partaker of it." In the Scripture text given as proof for the above words, I found more than 20 verses in all. But the one of special significance to me read, "And hereby we do know that we know Him if we keep His commandments" (I John 2:3). Now I knew why the Rev. John Newton agonized; he was waiting for confirming grace to enable him to keep the Commandments. Just as the drunkard must wait to be made sober before his heart can rest at peace, so all sinners must know they are being delivered from the practice of sin.

Here was the universal Biblical proof of salvation, not ecstatic spiritual experiences, visions, voices, or even soothing words from clerics. The Lord's gospel is given from above and confirmed by fruit for it is written, "By their fruits ye shall know them." I thought within myself, "No, I was certainly not perfect, but I was indeed far less of a constant sinner than I once was." I had hope that was based upon this change that was taking place in my life, and this was the hope that would never make me ashamed or disappointed, knowing that my salvation was genuine. Like Newton, grace relieved my fears, and I was free to press toward spiritual maturity.

## The Gospel of the Midas Touch

This is the gospel that you, dear reader, must teach if you are to have the Midas touch spoken of in Psalm 1, "And whatsoever he toucheth shall prosper." The Scotch-Irish drunks were genuinely in grace, because they were compelled to wait for deliverance from drunkenness before they could claim to be born again. Ordinary sinners, on the other hand, have been allowed in our permissive modern age to believe their prayer for salvation is effective without sin's yoke being broken from their necks. Ordinary sinners often continue to break their debt contracts, their marriage contracts, their obligations to their families, and blaspheme the name of Christ by claiming, or more accurately, presuming their salvation, while still in slavery to their besetting sins.

The Lord Jesus Christ is the only person with total free will. We ask Him to save, because only He can choose to redeem us. We know His answer is "yes" when we experience the power to overcome our sins. Until and unless we gain this power, we dare not assume that we are saved. Jesus saves, not us. It is the author's belief that this is the reason the modern church cannot transform our society. Believing that we can wish our salvation without confirming grace to stop sinning has removed the "fear of God" from our eyes. Without this fear, we do not learn. "The fear of the Lord is the beginning of wisdom" (Prov. 9:10). As Christian teachers, our responsibility is to lead our little children to wisdom.

At Grace Community, we teach the Bible teachers to say this, "Children, we have just asked Jesus to come into our hearts and save us. How will we know if Jesus is in our hearts? We can't see Him with our eyes, can we? Well, then, how will we know?"

The children know to answer the rhetorical question this way: "We will know when Jesus helps us to obey His commandments. When we find ourselves obeying father, mother, and teachers better and better, then we know Jesus is with us." Isn't this exactly what the word of God teaches?

I was still years away from developing the Grace Community system, but you won't have to wait years if you pay prayerful attention to these words and apply the operational manual that is advertised in the back of this book.

# CHAPTER XI
# A Better Gospel

The most compelling reason to found a Christian school is not financial gain, or security for your family, or freedom from being arbitrarily fired, or financial security in your old age, or even an inheritance for your children's children; the best and most Biblical of reasons for your Christian school is that you can instill a gospel that is not watered down. Matthew 6:33 states, "Seek ye first the Kingdom of God and His righteousness and all these things shall be added unto you." This formula for success is quite different from "Seek ye first profits measured in dollars." Matthew 6:33 is saying to seek first to extend the Kingdom of God and wealth is added as a by-product or an unintended consequence of first seeking to do our duty as designated by God. To the Christian school teacher, this means your first goal must be to capture as many young hearts for devotion and conversion to Godly living as possible. Happily, my system allows a stronger, purer, and more potent form of the gospel to be taught than would be possible in 99 percent of the churches or church schools in the world. I can best illustrate this gospel by asking you a Bible quiz question.

You are seating on a bench at Disney World. Toward you is strolling a buxom 16-year-old female. As she passes, you see a white patch framed in red, sewn to the seat of her skintight blue jeans. You notice the patch is shaped like a Valentine heart.

Inside the patch is some blue lettering. The lettering is hard to read, bouncing up and down and side to side, but presently you decipher the message. It reads, "God is Love," and below that, "I John 4:8." Puzzled, you read from your pocket testament, "He that loveth not, knoweth not God; for God is love."

Question: Please choose one of the following as most likely to have the greatest sin:

a. The buxom teen
b. Her pastor
c. Her parents
d. You! (Bible study on hinder parts, especially underage girls' parts, is "risky.")

Seriously, let's consider the first three choices and try to laugh about the fourth. I think we can agree that if the teenager confuses God's love with sex, she's a sinner. The Bible distinguishes between "good sex" such as lawful enjoyment of the marriage bed and unlawful or "bad sex" such as fornication and adultery. God's love, as defined by I John 5:2, is a quality that causes us to prefer the lawful and hate the unlawful. The teenager, like nearly all of her generation, probably lumps all sex together, and all love as romantic. The Bible, on the other hand, divides the clean from the unclean. The clean is known by its fruits or results. For example, we read in I John 5:3, "For this is the love of God, that we keep His commandments: and His commandments are not grievous."

In everyday language, if we regard it as "grievous" to pass up the joys of unlawful sex and boring to be confined to the lawful variety, we are not on the narrow path to paradise. We may have prayed the "Sinner's Prayer" and sincerely believe that we are heaven bound, but our destination is Hell and shame. Matthew

7:7 is best understood, "Ask [keep on asking] and it shall be given unto you; seek [keep on seeking] and ye shall find; knock [keep on knocking], and it shall be opened unto you." If the Lord validates our faith with a new desire for obedience and a fresh hatred for sin, we then know the love of God. A teenager, therefore, blinded by lust is very far from the kingdom of God. If, however, our teen cannot see the difference between evil love and God's love, perhaps her pastor shares some guilt. This teenager may be assisted to an early grave by her pastor's ignorance or negligence. If so, is not one to whom much is given, much required (Luke 12:48)?

Perhaps item (b), the pastor, is our best choice for our quiz answer. Let's review that possibility. The gospel honored by most of today's pastors accepts any sinner's prayer as sufficient evidence to be recognized as a Christian. "Salvation by grace through faith plus nothing" is the dictum they live by in the kingdom of the local church. Salvation by "any faith" is what the people mistakenly believe; and by the silence of the pastors, no separation is made between "vain faith" (I Cor. 5:1,2) and "saving faith" (Eph. 2:8-10). The beautiful gospel of the Bible's faithful universal church is perverted by silence, and "vain faith" is substituted for "effectual faith." Teenagers who have never experienced a changed life believe that they are Christians when they are not. No one has taught millions like our buxom teen that the call on Jesus must be examined by its results. Small wonder that preacher's children and church kids have no fear of God before their eyes. At every sermon, the pastor removes the fear of God by teaching, "It's a sin to doubt your salvation." Instead, the fear of God should be taught by saying, "Only faith proven by a changed life is the real thing!" The fruit of a perverted church gospel is tearing apart church families. "Ye shall know them by their fruit" (Matt. 7:16). So, what do you think?

The pastor choice (b)? But wait! Can the parents transfer primary responsibility for their children's education to servants of the church and school?

Consider this: At every orthodox baptism, the parents swear to "Bring them [their children] up in the nurture and admonition of the Lord" (Eph. 6:4). The pastor and the church members are also bound, but only "to help" in this task. The oath, primarily, binds the father and mother with the responsibility to keep the vow or suffer frightful sanctions. For this reason, we read in I Timothy 5:8, "But if any provide not for his own, and specially for those of his own house, he hath denied the faith and is worse than an infidel." This clearly means the parents must ensure that the child is taught the "fear of God" (that's what admonition means). The parents must see that this "good fear" is not confused with the fear that leads to Hell (Rev. 21:8). The parents must see that the child learns the difference between faith and "vain faith." The parents must examine the child to find fruit that indicates the child knows the difference between romantic love and God's love. The parents may hire a church and school to aide them in this holy obligation. But if the "hirelings" abandon the children for paychecks, pensions, honorary doctorates, or responsibility, the parents are not "off the hook!" Sad to say, the greatest sin or the best choice in answer to our quiz question is no doubt, "The parents." Of course, if the parents choose, teach, and set the right example to glorify God and the child, in spite of the parents' best efforts, willfully rejects the faith, the hands of the parents are clean, and the child is on his own. This brings us to my "clean hands plan" in two parts.

First, you must teach the beautiful gospel of the Bible's universal church, instead of the modern gospel taught in nearly every evangelical church. Don't worry! The true gospel is not as unknown to you as you may think. As a matter of fact, your pastor and your fellow church members know and use a tried and proven technique to teach this gospel. They use it on one particular sinner—the drunkard. Isn't it time that the drunkard is not allowed to pass himself off as a Christian until his prayer is answered by the Lord? Only when he is transformed from a drunk to a sober person is the alcoholic permitted peace from hearing "The drunkard shall be turned into Hell."

Ordinary sinners, like your children, experience a watered-down gospel. This gospel robs many of their birthrights (see II John 6-8). In every "soul-winning" church of my knowledge, the most attractive, faithful Christians are converted drunks. The "fear of God" was used to drive them through the strait gate.

The formula seems to be Fear of God (Ps. 19:9 and Prov. 1:9) = Wisdom (Prov. 9:10) = Seeking, Asking, Knocking (Matt. 7:7) = Faith (Eph. 2:8-10) = Love of God (I John 5:2,3) = Confirming Fruit (II Peter 3:14-18). Remember this key thought and question: "Is your child in his natural condition just as lost as the drunk?" Please read I Cor. 6 for the answer, "Know ye not that the unrighteous shall not inherit the kingdom of God? Be not deceived; neither fornicators, nor idolaters, nor adulterers, nor effeminate, nor abusers of themselves with mankind, nor thieves, nor covetous, nor drunkards, nor revilers, nor extortioners shall inherit the kingdom of God." It is clear, painfully clear, that children who cannot obey the commandments better and better are not growing in grace. Using the fear of God, we must warn them to flee from the wrath to come. Until they can honor and obey lawful authority from mother, father, pastor, policeman, or teacher, they must not be allowed to condemn themselves by wicked presumption that their prayer for salvation has been heard. The only fear, wisdom, faith, and love that can save their souls is defined by the law-word of the Bible and known by Godly fruit. Accept no substitutes! As you love the drunk, so love your child!

Now to the second part of the parents' hand-washing plan. I left the church of my father over thirty years ago. The Lord honored my faith. All eight of my children, their families, and my grandchildren worship and attend classes at the church and school that grew out of my home church. Today that church founded in my living room sponsors six Christian schools. My family enjoys spiritual and material blessings beyond our dreams. I want that for you. You will know in unmistakable terms what to do. Insist on the Bible's gospel being taught! Either the church members will change, or they will force you out! Don't worry; you will be in the very best of company. Church history records that every successful national revival or conversion begins when the sinners drive the saints outside the camp (see Heb. 13:13). As Jude 19 tells us, "These be they who separate themselves, sensual, not having the Spirit." We are called "Reformed Christians," because historically we desired reform rather than separation. So when strong families are driven out from "respectable, approved churches and schools," the saints should count it all joy! Don't rob yourself of your birthright by trying to win the "respect" of sinners. "But seek ye first the kingdom of God, and His righteousness; and all these things shall be added unto you" (Matt. 6:33).

## More Examples of Gospel Fruit

What follows are real-life illustrations of the Bible's gospel. The testimony of a two or three-year-old within even a "dysfunctional" home when in the hand of the Holy Spirit is an amazing encouragement for those of us in the day-to-day work of the preschool ministry. I had only been in Christian preschool work a few months, when one of our parents buttonholed me near the school door with the following question, "Reverend, do you teach the Commandments to the children here at school?"

I knew the woman to be a devout Roman Catholic with three daughters; therefore, I replied without hesitation, "Why, of course!"

She smiled graciously and replied, "I thought so, and do you teach the children to shout them at the top of their voices?"

Again, I answered quickly, (but now wondering where this was leading) "Yes, the shouting helps to lend some excitement to the drill and helps to imprint the commandments on their memory."

"Do you teach the commandment on adultery?" she continued.

Now less quickly and more concerned, I answered, "Yes, but, of course, we don't get into details with children so young about the meaning of that commandment. We do teach the children that they must be faithful to their marriage vows beginning right now at the age of two or three; in other words, adultery is more than just being faithful to your husband or wife after marriage."

Now she smiled even more broadly, to my relief and told the following story: "The other evening while my husband was buried in his newspaper, my little girl stomped through the living room, hands and feet swinging high, yelling at the top of her voice, 'Thou shalt not commit adultery!' My husband jerked to consciousness, threw the paper to the floor, and with bulging eyes, spitted out, 'What in hell is this all about?' I stammered, 'Well, I guess it's the Christian school teaching the commandments.' My husband replied, 'But why that commandment?' and 'Did you put her up to that?'"

At this point, she giggled, patted me on the shoulder, turned and left the building, shouting, "Keep up the good work, Reverend!"

## The Holy Spirit Uses Children

Yes, the testimony of a preschooler in the hands of the Holy Spirit can be devastatingly effective. Another example that comes to mind was told to us by a mother returning from her father's funeral in Tennessee. She said that she and most of her relatives are all non-church members, and the funeral was a very sad and discouraging service. But when the pastor began to quote the Lord's Prayer, the congregation was startled to hear the high-pitched sound of a child's voice reciting the words along with the pastor. After the service, many members of the family complimented her on the education of her two-year-old daughter and related how they were blessed to hear her daughter's expression of faith. The little girl kept telling all who would listen that "Grandpa was just sleeping with Jesus."

Over the years we have had dozens of such funeral stories. This ministry, which I pray will be yours also, has power to reach into homes that no church can reach. We have also dozens of stories of churches we have blessed through the testimony of our students. For example, a local pastor told me that during a service he quoted from the Twenty-third Psalm. (The Twenty-third Psalm, the Lord's Prayer, and the Commandments are recited by our students twice daily.) Therefore, when one of our students heard the Twenty-third Psalm, the three-year-old immediately chimed in. Seeing the surprise of the church members, the pastor told me he decided to take advantage of the situation. He asked the child if he wished to come to the pulpit to say the words with him. Instantly he said, in the manner of some who are not yet experienced enough to have stage fright, "Yes." The child bounded up the platform. While the pastor held his microphone to the boy's mouth, the child quoted the Twenty-third Psalm perfectly with feeling to the emotional response of the church.

## Families Made Whole

All in all, we have had dozens of couples, who were living together, become embarrassed by their illegitimate children who asked sharp questions about the Commandments, and then the couples legalized their common-law marriages. We also have had dozens of baptisms, re-dedications, and renewals of commitment to Christian doctrine. Again, let me emphasize that these are families who attend no church, but have been softened to the reach of the gospel through their children. It always surprises me that evangelical churches will organize door-to-door visitations but will not consider offering a needed service that will bring hundreds of potential converts to the doors of the church without any expense to the church and even at a profit, provided they were to use my system as laid out in our operational manual.

The daycare ministry or a Christian school built from scratch with a resulting church ministry is the logical way to win souls in our time. Historically, the Sunday School, presently atrophied to one insipid hour of pious goo with a watered-down gospel on Sunday morning, was originally a robust reading school taught daily to slum children in London by Robert Raike. Our ministry is in the solid tradition of the original Sunday

School. What is called Sunday School today is a tattered remnant of a once-effective church tool. The design for new models for evangelism has always been in the mainstream of the genuine faith set free from institutional arthritis. For example, the great Wyclif designed a model to fit his age.

## The Wyclif Model

Throughout church history, renewal has ordinarily come by means of men and ministries "outside the camp" (Exodus 29:14). Because of deep-seated heresies or self-serving bureaucracy, revival, by necessity, prospers outside churches. New life flows from the Lord through men and ministries of the church universal (i.e., catholic), chosen and blessed for their special mission. After the elect return to lawful obedience, the revival is forced on the local church. Churchmen typically argue that God's work cannot be undertaken without their blessing, aid, or "approved ordination." They are wrong. The best of many historical examples of these "outside the camp ministries" was the Lollards, founded and organized by the great Oxford educator, Wyclif (1320-1384). Wyclif's ministry had three characteristics common to most genuine revivals. First, it was a Biblical revival, not an emotional bath; second, it was funded without dependence on apostates; and third, his message was delivered in spite of, and independent of, the local church. The author has founded a 1990's version of Wyclif's model.

It is important to note that Biblical revival is much more than walking down a church aisle. Biblical revival is a return to obedience to God's law, instead of an emotional bath. (Definition: emotional bath is when you feel clean from sin, but your dirty sins remain, and worse, your ability to improve is less, not more! See Matt. 12:43-45). Wyclif taught the law as all those who reconstruct society must. Wyclif was a true evangelist. As R. J. Rushdoony, in his *Institutes of Biblical Law, Vol. I*, page 1, insightfully observes, "Wyclif's departure from accepted opinion was that the people themselves should not only read and know that law [referring to Biblical law], but also should in some sense govern as well as be governed by it." Our task is no different today. As true children of Wyclif, we must find a way to teach the elect that the laws and methods of democracy are not the laws and methods of God. We must also teach that a profession of faith not followed by a resulting obedience to the Commandments is not salvation or revival, but "the hope that maketh ashamed." The Christian school is a way to accomplish such a task, but most Christian schools are financially dependent on the erring church. If the law-word of God is to be taught, independent funding must be found. We of necessity must fund our work and fashion our tactics in spite of a church hooked on democracy and a humanistic plan of salvation and revival.

In order to accomplish this goal, Wyclif commissioned lay preachers to teach the law of God to the people in their own language. Financial support came only from the people served, not the establishment. God blessed and we now hail the school teacher Wyclif as "the morning star of the reformation." We rightly condemn the misguided churchmen who dug up his bones 10 years after his death as those "filthy dreamers [who] defile the flesh, despise dominion and speak evil of dignities" (Jude 8).

When we pray for revival, whether we are aware of it or not, we are asking for new ministries that will be viciously hated by the condemned but dearly loved by the blessed. Our school/daycare ministry is funded solely by the sale of daycare and education for children from infant and up. What's so revolutionary about that? First, we start from scratch without the aid of the church; second, we teach binding law; and third, we are able to deliver our doctrine directly to the elect. In other words, we follow the Wyclif model. Since 1986, six such schools have been founded. These schools provide a living wage and opportunity for those willing to labor beyond the pale of a mainline denomination. In fact, the wages are much more than those normally paid by the enemies of Christian reconstruction. The funding is secured by the free market. It is the author's pleasure to report that the profit from the sale of our services has freed our ministry from all dependence on gifts. We are expanding so fast that we are seeking men and women who are committed to Christian reconstruction to hire, provided they are committed to genuine Biblical salvation and revival. Our schools have prospered without a dime of tithe or freewill offerings. As a matter of corporate policy, 100 percent of our tithes and offerings must go to other ministries. In addition, our managers can be disciplined and dismissed for begging favors or money from our clients. We recognize that a ministry called to Christian reconstruction cannot prosper while depending on the good will, money, or tolerance of antinomians. So, like Wyclif, we have an independent core of teachers and independent support. But what about the message and its delivery?

### Waiting Until Six is Forbidding Children to Come

In order to benefit from Wyclif's genius, the correct audience must be taught with the correct message or we miss the mark. For that reason, we prefer to teach two-year-olds, instead of six-year-olds. Besides the obvious business consideration of serving a huge and growing demand for daycare for children of working mothers, the best window of opportunity to teach the law of God with the most impact is to teach little children. "Forbid them not!" warned our Lord, and on this point, even the social scientist agrees. A person's basic values are formed between the ages of two and five, simultaneously with learning the native tongue. The Christians, who wait for five or six-year-olds to start to try to win souls, have missed the boat! By refusing to offer a Christian alternative to the humanistic daycare, they have forbidden the children the opportunity to come to Christ. The best of all mission fields is now, and always has been, young children. From the preschool, reconstructionists can permit the elementary, secondary, and college to grow. Eventually, should the Lord bless, our graduates will feed into the local church demanding that God's Bible be regarded a binding law. True revival thus comes, simply, and logically.

Now, what to teach? Space won't permit full development, but the fear of God must be introduced if Christian education is to begin ("The fear of the Lord is the beginning of wisdom: and the knowledge of the holy is understanding" Prov. 9:10). The death, burial, and resurrection of Jesus, the Ten Commandments, yes of course, but most important, followed by this invitation designed to provoke wholesome fear of God, "How will we know if Jesus is our Shepherd? Let us pray right now that Jesus will bless you. If the Lord chooses to be your Shepherd, He will lead you in the paths of righteousness." (We have found the Twenty-third Psalm fits perfectly as a Biblical salvation prayer.) After the prayer, the rhetorical question should be asked repeatedly, "How will we know if Jesus is our Shepherd? Yes, He will help us to keep the Commandments." Don't bother to teach against any particular error. Since you have "first crack" at these children, you have no need to contradict error. Let the heretics try to teach these children as they grow older that Christians have no need for supernatural obedience to validate their profession of faith.

I have faith that easy-believism will fail. Our school has discovered that even nominal Christian parents are very pleased to learn that their children know the Commandments, the Lord's

Prayer, and the Twenty-third Psalm. Very, very seldom have we had any complaint about this approach. The door is wide open!

## Do You Have Zeal?

Several years ago, when my first school was only five years old, I founded a franchising corporation with a vision of starting Christian schools like a McDonald's or similar franchising arrangement. What I discovered was that those who had the money to buy a franchise almost always lacked the necessary zeal to win souls as their first desire; those, on the other hand, who had the vision of Matt. 6:33 to extend first the dominion of Christ almost always lacked investment capital. This has led me to make the following offer:

I will offer employment to qualified applicants with or without a college degree—home school graduates welcome, converted single parents welcome also; in short, nearly anyone who has the proper religious zeal to desire an apprenticeship to learn our system is welcome. We only require that you sign a non-compete agreement to not start a school within 40 miles of one of our present schools. This is a very generous offer, because it allows you to acquire or, more accurately, "steal" all of my trade secrets while earning a salary.

My other offer would be that if you think you already have the necessary experience or you have a ministry under your control that you wish to convert to a profit maker, I will sell you my manual. Your only obligation would be to sign a legal agreement not to reprint and sell the manual. In this manner, everyone reading this book should pray earnestly about themselves, their children, their grandchildren, or associates as potential candidates for becoming school owners who will have all the earthly benefits of being a business owner, but also the vast treasures in heaven that only such a ministry can yield. How much reward can be earned? Well, the Bible says that if a man gains the entire world but loses his soul, he has made a bad trade. In other words, the soul of a child won is worth all the treasure of earth. In my former days, I was a commissioned salesman. What do you suppose the commission would be on a sale valued at more money than all the treasures of the world? Well worth pursuing, don't you agree?

As I finish this book, I am seated in a penthouse apartment overlooking Pelican Bay in Naples, Florida. The ads regularly appear in New York newspapers advertising Pelican Bay as "The best the world has to offer." In other words, my friend, my potential soul-winning Christian school teacher/friend, if my reward in heaven is not worthy to be compared with this "earnest" down payment of a penthouse apartment and owner-ship of six school buildings and four faculty houses and on and on, then the size of the heavenly reward is immense. I want that for you. Write to me today and let's discuss your rewards on heaven and earth. The Lord Jesus Christ pays His faithful servants very well indeed. After all, didn't He promise to divide the spoil with the strong? May God bless you as you consider this Wyclif model for the 1990s and the coming century.

## CHAPTER XII
## Conclusion

All of the preceding builds precept upon precept to this: you can own your own private school and enjoy financial independence in this life and reap an eternal reward in the next life by following my system. You must know or learn to know that freedom and that owning and controlling private property are one and the same. You must know how to be or learn to be an effective parent as well as a teacher to your students. You must succeed at recruiting a student body from advertising similar to our direct mail program. You must choose the right location. You must avoid the discredited reading and math programs of the government schools. You must present the gospel with more power than churches that support public education.

Your calling as a Christian teacher is complex. You must teach the young by precept and example how to live for Christ. Such a huge task cannot be finished with a tract describing four simple steps. "He that winneth souls is wise" (Prov. 11:30). If you are compassionate, wise, soul-winning teacher, you know in your heart that the whole counsel of the word of God should be taught to children before they face this world—the younger the better! This is your holy task. If so (and it is), you will be rewarded for intelligently executing your calling and punished with loss if you do not.

Because I am a God-called teacher as well as you, I know you are willing to sacrifice. I dragged my family through an unnecessary hell, because I had more zeal than knowledge. That's just fine if it has to be that way. But does it? So, I was called to teach, but was I justified in jeopardizing my family's happiness and future to satisfy my misguided doctrine? Perhaps if it was absolutely, positively the only way, but you, fellow teacher/soldier, do not have to crawl through that mine field without my map! There is an easier way.

Is it God-honoring and wise to stake your family's security and your old age on the managerial ability of the local church or Christian school? Is it prudent? May I suggest that my way is less risky? Consider for a moment that I have founded six schools and set forth their detailed procedures in my operational manual. Banks do not lend money to risky ventures. In fact, money is very difficult to obtain for start-up ventures in even boom times. My success is your assurance that my program works.

On the other hand, what is your alternative? Let's say the worst possible event occurs—you go bankrupt! What then? Couldn't you find another job as good or nearly as good as the one you have? Sure, you may lose, but remember that a loss can happen right in your present situation as well. Wrapping a gift in a napkin and burying it in the ground (school) won't be worth much at the judgment seat. Read Luke 19.

Consider the freedom to reach hundreds of souls in a most effective manner. Consider the freedom to teach the best and truest reading program free from bureaucratic bungling. Consider the freedom to own and teach the truth. Consider the double honor and double pay of being a self-employed professional; leap over the high wall when you see yourself expanding the dominion of the Lord Jesus Christ. The men I introduced to my school system are in the top 1 percent of the nation's wage earners. I take pleasure in the peace in their eyes when they praise the Lord for His calling. Their success is my success; your success is important to me.

If you have a family, your children will have your shoulders to stand on as they add to the inheritance you lay up for them. Really now, does the government deserve to be your heir or does the fruit of your life of labor belong to your flesh and blood? How much of your pension will be paid to your children?

Your clientele of parents and children are willing to pay you a magnificent income and an estate for your children if you can meet their needs for quality daycare and education in a free market. Is that fair? Of course, it is. They are willing to enter into voluntary tuition contracts to buy your ministry. As parents, they are charged by the law of God with training their children in the nurture and admonition of God. They need you, Christian teacher, to carry out their solemn duty to educate their children. Just as a lawyer or medical doctor enters the market to meet a need, so can you as a professional educator.

## Why Must You Have a Manual?

I know that most teachers who read these words will ask themselves, "Do I need to buy a manual?" The more experience you have, the more likely you are to believe that you can start and operate a successful business without a manual. You are wrong, and I can prove it.

First, ask yourself this question, "How many people do you know who have started a business from scratch?" Of these, how many are earning the level of income I am discussing? Very few.

Why? Because starting a successful anything from zero is a very difficult task that requires skills 99 percent of teachers do not possess. Let me recommend a book that will develop that fact for you. It is called *The E-Myth* by Michael E. Gerber (Ballinger Publishing Co., Cambridge, Mass., 1986). Gerber's thesis is that the reason almost all start-up businesses fail is because the skill to pull off the task is rare. Nearly all businesses are started by technicians lacking in entrepreneurial ability. Therefore, you, dear reader, will very likely never be able to start a successful enterprise. But wait! Ever see a McDonald's fast food restaurant? Of course, you have; there are thousands of McDonald's managed by people who also lacked entrepreneurial skills. What is their secret? The McDonald's operational manual. The entire franchise system has stood the business start-up success ratio on its head. Instead of most start-up businesses failing, the reverse becomes true via a manual, because all businesses are basically systems. The entrepreneur is the composer of the system. He has the creative talent to produce something new, if the system is completely described. With written music, any musician can capture Mozart. Only Mozart, however, could compose Mozart's music, but with written music, lesser mortals can play beautiful music. Vary from Mozart's written instructions far enough, and you have noise and failure, not music.

## As in Music, So in Business

You must have the manual to make the business succeed. There are probably scores of church-run daycare/preschools in your town. Perhaps your church operates such a facility. Perhaps your child attends a Christian school. Are they yielding a generous profit to their owners? "No" is the correct answer. Why? It is because they don't have a successful system. Don't you imagine they would succeed if they could? What kind of school could you produce without a system? You have experience, you say?

Well, if you worked for one of those losing schools, you know a system that loses, not how to make a success.

Let's say you know someone who manages to make a profit. Can he tell you how he does it? It is probable that he cannot! Talent does the task by using talent. It's instinctive. Not only must the successful entrepreneur demonstrate his success, but his system also has to be captured and transmitted to you, so that you can duplicate his system. Without this, my friend, you may have only bankruptcy at the end of your efforts.

Fortunately, there is a better way. It removes trial and error. Remember: even if you are possessor of entrepreneurial skills (and you may be), there is still costly trial and error. Even with lots of talent, you may run out of money, making correction after correction, searching for the working formula. Perhaps you can stumble through, but why do that when my manual is available to you at less cost than one tiny trial and error mistake?

At the beginning of this book, I said, "I pray you will learn from this book how the yoke (of oppression) can fall from you." Now, I am a serious Christian. When I said, pray, I mean just that, PRAY. When a serious Christian prays, he must back up his prayer by Godly action; otherwise, he is not a serious Christian. I will sell you my system, because I want the Godly reward for thousands of children you will affect for Christ in His kingdom.

## So, You Have an Education

Matt 25:30, "And cast ye the unprofitable servant into outer darkness: There shall be weeping and gnashing of teeth." A Christian education should include two lessons for the sake of the testimony. For the past twenty years, I have had the responsibility of interviewing, hiring, training, and sometimes firing people with advanced college degrees. My conclusion, based on this experience, is that the least productive workers in our present world are those who are best educated in terms of credentials. If my opinion is unique, the reader can dismiss me as a grumpy old man. But to the disgrace of those laboring for the church, my opinion is widely held, because it is based on demonstrated fact, not illusion. Businessmen will extend credit faster to non-Christians than to pastors or churches, because those who deal in the marketplace know Christians to be, as a rule, "dead beats." Bankers are very reluctant to extend credit for a Christian ministry. Experience has taught them that such loans are "questionable." What is the lesson that should be taught in our Christian schools and seminaries? To fail to keep your credit contracts is to steal, to break the covenant, and to be an unprofitable servant.

There is a second lesson needed. The world, as ordered by God, rewards work more than words. Booker T. Washington, about a century ago, tried to protect his black students from the anti-Christian notion that a man "should live by his wits alone." Washington insisted that all his students, in order to graduate, had to be proficient in a marketable trade. Our seminaries and Christian colleges have produced hordes of graduates more ignorant than Washington's field-hand blacks in the realities of the marketplace. The marketplace rewards the manufacturer more than the inventor. The marketplace rewards the producer more than the writer. The marketplace rewards the successful trader more than the professor. The marketplace rewards the pastor who builds his church more than the pastor who vegetates in someone else's church. The marketplace rewards the teacher who owns, operates, and builds his school more than the teacher who teaches three classes per week in someone else's school. To make matters easier to grasp, God rewards demonstrated successful work over the best diploma from the best school. The profitable servant succeeds in the public market regardless of success in private markets called schools, colleges, and seminaries. Why do you suppose genius is so often found without a college degree? I suspect much genius is squashed, squelched, and killed by failing to understand the relatively useless value of a diploma without the will and ability to work. Why is it that most of the largest churches in America are built by men without a "proper Presbyterian education?" Could it be that what passes for a proper education fails to teach the absolute requirement to work?

I spend my time now searching for men and women who want to start Christian schools. My method is to start where the free market is most ready to accept a new school (i.e., the daycare field). From a profitable daycare, a hard-working family can easily earn $50,000 a year. From that daycare center, students can be retained for higher and higher grades until a solid, profitable school can be built. Hundreds of souls can be saved, and the whole counsel of God taught without interference from a church board or denominational religious bigotry. It is a proven financial and spiritual winning plan, but... and it's a huge BUT... most of the "educated" Christians I talk to regard starting at the preschool level as beneath their lofty station. "I am 'not called to that,'" they say. After they discover that they must work all year long without a three-month summer vacation or a legion of holidays, and horror, more than six to eight hours a day, well, that is just not their calling, you see. Yes, sadly, I do see just as Booker T. Washington saw his blacks, "Such are not profitable." Much of the blame can be laid at the door of our Christian educational experience.

Happily, I have found a solution to my dilemma. Preschools do not require college credentials, so I have begun to hire non-degreed individuals who want to work to establish a career that will pay more than a pastor and a school teacher's salary combined.

Here's an idea that several families are taking advantage of right now at Grace Community Schools. Instead of sending their high school graduates to colleges for four years of questionable education, they are sending their children to Grace Community for a three-year apprenticeship program. We provide housing and a good salary while they learn our system. At the end of the three years, their families can take the money they would have invested in a college education and use that money instead to set up their children in their own business. Doesn't that make a lot of sense? This is the approach I have used for six of my eight children. They stayed home and apprenticed with me, taking college courses for an external degree from a Christian university. This way they earn a degree in the academic world. But more importantly, they have developed the business skills to be financially independent for the rest of their lives. Therefore, why stand ye idle?

EPILOGUE

# Godly Spouses Wanted

The first Grace Community School founded by Rev. Ellsworth McIntyre and his family opened on February 3, 1986.

Since then, the McIntyre family has followed God's command to "be fruitful and multiply." Now thirty-five years later, most of Rev. and Mrs. McIntyre's seventy-plus children, grandchildren, and great-grandchildren have stayed in the Southwest Florida area working for the current Grace Community School locations and planning the future ones.

The end result of all this is that we have a surplus of godly Christian men and women of marriageable and soon-to-be-marriageable age seeking Christian spouses to be helpmeets in their missionary callings here at Grace Community School.

These children have been raised in Grace Community Schools and homeschooled by their parents, away from public schools and secular colleges.

More than that, they have learned the trade of operating Christian schools in all aspects, including management, teaching, and finances. From the youngest of ages, they begin to help us with our school's day-to-day operations. When they are sixteen years of age, they officially become employees of our school as teacher assistants. For one year, they learn how to work in and operate a classroom and teach children reading, writing, and arithmetic. When they are seventeen, they begin to help manage classrooms, learn how to handle staff planning and support, and overall building management and routines. When they are eighteen, they start working on staff management, public relations, sales, accounting, and business management. During these three years, they will also complete all degrees and certifications that they need to operate a private Christian school. When they turn nineteen, they are given a position as an assistant director of a Christian school and put all of the skills they have learned over the past three years into practice. At twenty-one years of age, they can become director of a private Christian school, overseeing all aspects of it to ensure its proper management. These three years are what we call the "Grace Community School Apprenticeship Program." For our children, there is more.

During the entirety of their financial career, our children are encouraged to save a minimum of fifty percent of their income, excluding their tithe. This lets them build the financial means to begin a family in the future and shows their responsibility and suitability as a prospective spouse. None of their peers can match this advantage. Not only is this a massive help in starting a family, but it also gives them the necessary discipline of forethought frugality that is needed to care for a family.

Grace Community School, along with their skills and proficiency in business and personal discipline, provides these young men and women with everything they need to have a financially prosperous and stable future.

All that they lack is a spouse that can work alongside them in their calling as Christian educators and missionaries to their community. This is what we are looking for: helpmeets that will enable them to fulfill their calling of evangelism and discipleship of the local community and let them rear a Godly family to the glory of God and the extension of His kingdom.

All too many modern Christians seem to have a sad lack of desire to form Godly marriages. We at Grace Community School and the GCS Apprenticeship Program want to make long-lasting family connections. We are looking for Godly families who have children looking for spouses, who have a heart for evangelism, and who understand the importance of Godly marriages and families. Are you interested? Do you know someone who is? We want to talk to you! Email us at: gcsapprenticeship@gmail.com

# The Grace Community School Apprenticeship Program

The GCS Apprenticeship Program is seeking out men and women who want to make a difference in their communities and in the lives of others. Apprentices acquire the credentials, tools, skills, and knowledge needed to reform and reconstruct society from the bottom up via uncompromisingly Christian education.

Grace Community School is a missions operation unlike any other. Our apprentices learn to operate sustainable, self-supporting Christian schools ministering to those in our society who need it most: young children, many of whom are spiritual orphans. We are devoted to bringing the Gospel to the underprivileged and needy in our community.

Apprentices learn to operate successful Christian schools via fun and interactive on-the-job training under proven senior school operators. If you want to experience the joys of worthwhile work advancing God's Kingdom and learning practical skills while enriching the lives of children, the Grace Community School Apprenticeship Program might be for you!

**Get books, articles, podcasts, and more at**
www.gcsapprenticeship.com

**Contact Us**

Email: gcsapprenticeship@gmail.com
Phone: (239) 234-2799
Mail: 8971 Brighton Lane, Bonita Springs, FL 34135

# More Books and Materials from Nicene Press and the Grace Community School Apprenticeship Program

**Preschool Pioneers Podcast**

The world needs Christian teachers. Join Jeremy Walker as he discusses why Christians should become teachers and gives practical advice to help Christians get inspired, get equipped, and get involved in Christian education.

Visit cr101radio.com/preschoolpioneers/ our search for Preschool Pioneers on Apple Podcasts, Spotify, Google Podcasts, or wherever else podcasts can be found.

## *A Full Reward: Reformation Through Family-Run Christian Schools* by Rev. Aaron M. Slack

Christianity is in crisis. The world is nowhere near where it should be and seems to be getting worse. As our culture and society free fall further into degeneracy, the question is asked: what are we to do?

Conscientious Christians, knowing that we are called to be salt and light in this earth, are making efforts. What has emerged is an emphasis on politics, apologetics, and evangelism at the adult level. *A Full Reward: Reformation Through Family-Run Christian Schools* is a look at something different.

Current efforts at reformation have had mixed results. *A Full Reward* offers a new hope. The book's thesis is this: reformation will come, but it will come from the bottom up, via ministry to the youngest members of our society: our preschool children.

Get the book on Amazon Kindle or wherever eBooks are sold.

# Grace Community School Curriculum and Operations Manual

## Grace Community School Operations Manual

The GCS Operations Manual is a complete guide in how to operate a Christian school. The GCS business model has been developed over 33 years and has proven to be successful.

## College Can Begin at 2 Preschool Curriculum

A full preschool curriculum appropriate for ages 2-5 years of age. Everything a school needs to operate a sustainable, fun, exciting, and educational preschool program.

### Grace Community School Reading Program

A complete beginners phonics reading program including learning materials and audio and video files.

### Grace Community School Math Program

A complete beginners math program including flip books and certificates.

## Grace Community School Bible Program

A complete Bible program that will help any school create a complete preschool Bible program.

## Preschool in a Box

All of the above books, materials, and more in one convenient package! **Visit gcsapprenticeship.com/materials/ for more information and to purchase.**

www.ingramcontent.com/pod-product-compliance
Lightning Source LLC
LaVergne TN
LVHW050720250326
834741LV00050B/1111